<small>UNDERSTANDING</small>
GOD'S CONTRACTS WITH MANKIND
SECOND EDITION

Understanding
God's
Contracts
with Mankind

Second Edition

Your Path to
Understanding Christianity

J. William Howerton

Understanding God's Contracts with Mankind: Your Path to Understanding Christianity
Second Edition

Copyright © 2022 by J. William Howerton. All Rights Reserved.

For information about this title or to order other books and/or electronic media, contact the publisher:

J.William Howerton
blhow@comcast.net

Library of Congress Control Number: 2022912004

ISBNs:
979-8-9862130-0-2 (hardcover)
979-8-9862130-1-9 (softcover)
979-8-9862130-2-6 (eBook)
979-8-9862130-3-3 (audiobook)

Printed in the United States of America

Cover and Interior design: 1106 Design

DEDICATION

This book is dedicated to:

My Lord and Savior, Jesus Christ, without whom this book would not have been possible, needed, or relevant.

My wife, Eva, who has done so much to guide me and encourage me in my Christian walk.

My parents, Nell and Walter Howerton, who had me in church and Sunday school every week from the time of the cradle roll through senior high classes; and, especially to my father who was, indeed, a self-made Bible scholar. Unfortunately, we do not always appreciate what we have until it is too late.

My cousin, and dear close friend, Jane Carson Myre, who exposed me to outstanding Christian laymen, leaders, pastors, teachers, evangelists, and events, and to Christian books and audio and video lessons. She never let up or gave up.

My children, John, Jane, and Clay, and my stepchildren, Kurt, Kim, and Eric, who provided an excellent motivating reason for me to regain my interest in Christianity and church activities.

And finally, to all my friends who put up with me and helped guide me in Bible studies, retreats, and various Christian learning experiences.

My Thanks and Love to All.

✝

TABLE OF CONTENTS

†

INTRODUCTION FOR THE "SECOND EDITION"

There are at least three relevant questions which demand answers. Why a second edition? What is new? What has changed?

When the book was first published in 2015, I had no idea there would be a need to update the content. However, another series of events became highly significant involving my "personal relationship." It was compelling enough to motivate me to republish and add the story. You will find it as a new section D in chapter 6, entitled "The Rest of the Story."

The idea of the rapture and its timing remains a hotly debated and controversial subject. While I still have no opinion to set in concrete, I have done some serious rethinking of my position and have chosen to rewrite that portion of the book. Perhaps it will be a little clearer, or at least identify where the confusion remains. This section will again be found in Section C of chapter 8 entitled, "Some Thoughts on the Rapture and Its Timing."

The Epilogue has been rewritten and updated, and Appendix C in the first edition has been eliminated. Otherwise, except for a few tweaks to update, or clarify where needed, the overall text remains the same.

Finally, let me urge you not to skip the preface and acknowledgments chapter. It not only allows me to introduce myself, but it also identifies my primary individual sources. Importantly, near the end of that chapter is a quote and story that generally sets up a theme for the book: "The development of your soul."

†

PREFACE AND ACKNOWLEDGMENTS

"And the things you have heard me say in the
presence of many witnesses entrust to reliable people
who will also be qualified to teach others."
2 TIMOTHY 2:2

(All citations will be from the *New International*
Version, unless otherwise noted.)

Have you ever hit a hole-in-one, a grand slam home run, or caught a really big fish? If you did, you wanted to talk about it. Well, that's how I felt when I had a genuine encounter with the Holy Spirit. Starting about 1971 Eva and I attended, among other Bible studies, a lengthy session on gifts of the Holy Spirit primarily covering chapter 12 of 1 Corinthians. Other studies had to do with the gifts and fruits of the Spirit, and administrations within the Church. I had not had any particular personal relationship which many people talk about, nor had I knowingly received gifts of the Holy Spirit. Nine are identified and of course the gift of faith is one of them. Perhaps when I first believed, I received that gift of faith. Two other gifts are a word of knowledge and a word of wisdom. I am now aware of these two, and sincerely believe that I have experienced both. (A word of knowledge or wisdom is not all knowledge or wisdom, but just what one might need at a specific time).

At the time I now refer to, I was working as city manager in the city of Paducah, but also maintaining a law practice. One of the clients was a bank which provided various legal work of all types. On a particularly busy day when I probably had a phone in each ear and someone was asking me questions from across the desk, I received a call from the bank advising me that for the board meeting that afternoon they would like to have a resolution honoring a person that was very dear to the bank. I almost panicked when I thought of getting the document prepared in time, so I said I will write something and bring it to you, but you will have to type it up for me.

It was near noon, and as soon as the room cleared out, I shut the door, got out my legal pad and pen, paused to reflect a bit, but then prayed. While I cannot remember the prayer, what I generally asked was: "Lord, if there is such a thing as the Holy Spirit to work with us, and if there are such things as gifts of a word of knowledge or wisdom, I need help now." What happened after that was that some peace and calm came over me and I began to write. Unlike most of the time when I scratch out something and change things around, what I needed to put on that paper went on it. As soon as I was able, I took it to the bank, and got it typed. At the meeting that afternoon, when they were reading the resolution, someone asked who wrote it, and somebody said that Bill wrote it. I just smiled a little bit and nodded affirmatively. At that time, I thought to myself that I ought to tell the truth about this and what really happened. However, I naturally did not. I will talk more about other experiences, when I get to the chapter on the Holy Spirit.

As Eva and I began to grow more and more in our faith and understanding and in knowledge of the Word of God, we participated in several weekend activities by invitation. I gave my testimony, and she gave hers at functions such as "Faith Alive," an activity of the Episcopal Church.

In 1976 I was elected to the Court of Appeals of Kentucky, which is a story in itself. (I will tell a few things about the election also in the chapter on the Holy Spirit.) Shortly after the election, we were invited to attend a Full Gospel Businessmen Fellowship dinner in Paducah. We had the privilege of sitting with Mr. and Mrs. A.A. Boone of Nashville, Tennessee. We had a great visit and conversation, and Mrs. Boone asked me if I knew anything about the Blood Covenant. I told her that I did not, and she offered to send me some tapes on that subject. She did. There were six of them by a Bible expositor, teacher, or evangelist whose name was Malcolm Smith. Unfortunately, I no longer have those tapes, but I certainly listened to them many times. I used them to help in my early research. I just wish there was some way at this time that I could tell Mrs. Boone that her sending them to me was not in vain.

As I write later, there will be times when I will be passing ideas I learned from those tapes by Malcolm Smith, but I cannot make any specific reference or specific quotes. So just know that much of what I pass on to you now I learned from the things he said on those tapes. They were on the Blood Covenant between Abraham and God and about the blessings and curses that went along with the Covenant.

Now might also be a good time to mention that in the early 1980s I had begun a study of the three annual Convocations and Seven Feasts required of the Jewish people. I found some tapes by a minister or teacher named Rick Godwin from San Antonio, Texas. I learned a lot from studying those tapes, so again there will be times in this book when I refer to those required feasts and what they meant. I should be giving credit to Rick Godwin, but cannot, so I am doing it this way now to say that much of what you may learn through me I learned through him. Otherwise throughout this writing I expect to make some citations which will be put in an index at the end of the book. Direct quotes from the Bible will be cited as they are presented and included in text form in the pages of this book.

I must also give credit to Dr. J. T. Parish, pastor and founder of Christian Fellowship Church and school in Briensburg, Kentucky, who over a period of six or eight weeks lectured our Bible study group on the Holy Spirit. Much of what I write about in chapter 6 on the manifestations of the Spirit, I learned from his lectures and subsequent study. I use the term "manifestations" rather than merely "gifts," as there are not only gifts, but "fruits of the Spirit" and "administrations" for the Church. My thanks to Dr. Parish for a good jump-start on understanding and getting to "know" the Holy Spirit in a more personal way.

If I might digress for a moment, this would be a good time to mention that although I had heard of having a "personal relationship" with God, when I was growing up what I heard about was Father, Son, and Holy Ghost. Had I known of the concept of the Holy Spirit and His gifts, things would have undoubtedly been different in my life. I mainly dismissed the idea of a "Ghost" as if there was only God and Jesus. Keep in mind that it is the Holy Spirit that is God in us. You might recognize the Spirit as your conscience, as you will be convicted as you commit sin. The Spirit is Holy, and we are expected to be Holy while the Spirit lives in us. Impossible, perhaps, but that is the goal, nevertheless.

While thinking about writing this book, I originally thought I had a fairly simple task. However, the more I delayed and put it off, the more I learned. It really became difficult to determine what to write and what to leave out. I hated to leave out anything, but there is no way I can include everything. Whatever, many authors have covered these other subjects far better than I ever could, so I am going to stick to the core theology that I have learned. I want to pass on enough information to people to help them *understand* what Christianity is all about. I will simply give references in an appendix identifying specific books which should be helpful.

I should also mention that while serving on the court and as chief judge, I was invited to attend a conference at the Institute of Basic Life Principles' North Woods Conference Center in Upper Michigan. I was privileged to do that for two years. The first year featured as the primary presenter David Barton of Wall Builders in Aledo, Texas. While much of what he presented certainly had a Christian background to it, he was concentrating on the Christian influence on America's founders and the founding of The United States of America. I very well may refer to certain things concerning our government, where we were and where we are now, which would be based on sources I learned from Barton.

One thing I will include as an appendix to this book is an opinion I wrote in 1993 which is somewhat of a political science and history lesson, but much of what is presented in the opinion I learned at that conference. The only thing I can say in addition to that is that anything I used from Barton, I was able to obtain the actual source of a book, or magazine or whatever, and those citations were given in the opinion. I believe those four will be the only broad credits that I need to give for source material that will be in this book.

One other source that has been important to me has been Charles Colson. He has written numerous books, and to my knowledge I have most of them. From time to time, I will refer to some of his writing, but before getting into the real subject I want to mention one other quote which I find very profound and true. In his book *Loving God*[1]. Colson tells the story of the conversion of Aleksandr Solzhenitsyn. It is a wonderful story not only about the conversion of Solzhenitsyn but also about Dr. Boris Kornfeld whose example and comments led to Solzhenitsyn's conversion to Christianity. Colson writes:

> Boris Kornfeld is the great paradox personified. A Jew who betrayed the faith of his fathers. A doctor whose years of training were senselessly wasted. A political idealist whose utopian

vision led only to a barren Siberian prison. A prisoner who gave up his life for nothing more than a loaf of stolen bread. In every one of the areas, Boris Kornfeld was a failure—at least in the world's system of values. Yet God took that failure of a man and through his single-minded obedience used him to lead to Christ another who would go on to become a prophetic voice and one of the world's most influential writers.

For Kornfeld's words did their convincing, convicting work, touching what Solzhenitsyn later called "a sensitive chord." That was his moment of spiritual awakening; "God of the universe, I believe You again! Though I renounced You, You will be with me," he cried out. It was a spiritual transfusion—life taken from one man and pumped into another for God's sovereign purpose.

And in his conversion Solzhenitsyn saw clearly the kingdom paradox. For in the emptiness of that Russian gulag, he perceived what pleasure-seeking millions in the abundance of Western life cannot. He wrote later: "the meaning of the earthly existence lies, not as we have grown used to thinking, in prospering, but in the development of the soul."[2]

Indeed, the conclusion that *the real meaning of life is in the development of the soul* is most profound, and for the Christian, it must be true. Our earthly existence is brief, but eternity for the soul is forever. Eternity is unimaginable, but years ago, I heard or read a word picture which attempted to describe the idea. It compared eternity to a granite rock one hundred miles cubed. Nothing affected it except that one day each year a tiny bird would fly to the rock to sharpen its beak. When the rock was totally removed by this one cause only, eternity would still not be ended.

So, if you are a true believer, you must follow the teachings of Jesus Christ, and stick to the task of developing your soul. In the totality of everything, nothing could be more important.

One must understand that the Christian life is not such an easy life. In John 16, we read: "²⁴Then Jesus said to his disciples, "Whoever wants to be my disciple must deny themselves and take up their cross and follow me. ²⁵For whoever wants to save their life will lose it, but whoever loses their life for me will find it."

Also, in Matthew 24, at verse 9, Jesus was speaking to His disciples concerning the end of the age, and He said, "Then you will be handed over to be persecuted and put to death, and you will be hated by all nations because of me."

While I am not trying to scare anyone away, we must be aware that Christianity does have rules, or commandments, which must be kept. We know of the Ten Commandments, but Jesus summarized them into two, when responding to a question of which commandment was the greatest. In Matthew 22:37-40 we find:

> ³⁷Jesus replied: "Love the Lord your God with all your heart and with all your soul and with all your mind. ³⁸This is the first and greatest commandment. ³⁹And the second is like it: "Love your neighbor as yourself. ⁴⁰All the Law and the Prophets hang on these two commandments."

Let's face it, if you love your neighbor as yourself, you are not likely to be doing evil things to your neighbor. Your neighbor is everyone.

Jesus orders us to love Him, and to obey his commandments, and he promises the Holy Spirit to help us know and live by the rules. In Matthew 14, at verses 15-17, we learn:

> ¹⁵If you love me, keep my commands. ¹⁶And I will ask the Father, and he will give you another advocate to help you and be with you forever—¹⁷the Spirit of truth. The world cannot accept him

because it neither sees him nor knows him. But you know him, for he lives with you and will be in you.

However, it still will not be easy; human beings and the Kingdom of Earth are just not wired that way. The Kingdom of God is in constant conflict with our earthly ways and the spirits in control of this earth.

Many of us attend or have attended what I refer to as "happy church." We are told to believe, and we are saved. We hear little about the rules. Just show up, give your money, be happy, and all will be well in the by and by. Someday those that preach only cheap grace and easy salvation will be hated by those in the congregation who have never been told the hard truth about the hard times. Sure, we can be happy in Jesus, especially when we apply the truth to our relationship with Him and His commandments. It is a good way to live and develop the soul.

It is certainly not up to me to judge anyone's relationship with Jesus Christ, but I have a hard time believing that anyone who shows up at church perhaps four times in their life is ready for eternal life in the presence of God. By four times, I am referring to being brought in for baptism, forced to attend a confirmation class and receive Holy Communion, show up for a marriage ceremony, and then finally brought back for a burial service. Personally, I just do not believe that is sufficient faith and belief. You may think you know Jesus, but does he know you?

While I have no doubt that one who comes in at the last hour, and perhaps without baptism, can still be "saved," as in such situations the individual has found a true belief, sincerely repents, and is sorry for the sins committed throughout his life, and desires to convert and change his ways to become a follower of Jesus Christ. We can know this from the convict who was crucified beside Christ, and was promised "paradise" that very day, and from the parable of the workers in the vineyard. Those who came to work last, or at the eleventh hour, received the same pay or reward as those who began "laboring in the vineyard" early in the day. See Matthew 20, verses 1-16.

Clearly, I do not have all the answers. I am just a beggar who has found some bread, and desires to share it. I do hope to give a good overview of what I believe Christianity is all about. I hope to help Christians *understand* and keep their faith through all times and tribulations, and to help the nonbelievers come to a realization that there is a God who is in charge and actually loves them and seeks a relationship with them. Remember, wrong choices could lead to eternal damnation. So, ask yourself, is the risk worth it? You might also ask yourself, if the Bible and Gospel are true, what do I have to lose? Living your life accordingly can and will be happy. Living the Christian life gives love, peace, and joy that cannot be obtained living a carnal life.

As is indicated by the title, we will be studying God's Contracts with Mankind. We will be looking at the more serious and lasting contracts, called "Covenants." The two main broad covenants in the Bible are the Old Covenant made with Abraham for his descendants through his son Isaac and Jacob (Israel), and the New Covenant made for all mankind between God and Jesus Christ. The Bible more commonly calls the New and Old Covenants, Testaments. We will look more closely at each in chapters 4 and 5. Keep in mind that you must understand the Old Covenant, together with the laws and requirements established through it, and the prophesies about Jesus, to understand how Jesus fulfilled those laws and prophesies and established the New Covenant.

Finally, I hope to make something perfectly clear. While I have used a lot of "I"s so far, this book is not about me, the writer. It is necessary to give some idea of my background and where I have obtained much of my information. Although there will be some more of such, I hope to hold it to a minimum. Of necessity, there will be some in chapter 1 and especially chapter 6, where I shed some light on the concept of a personal relationship with Jesus Christ and The Holy Spirit. Very definitely, however, this book is about God, and His relationship with humanity.

†

CHAPTER 1

WHY THIS BOOK?

*"Always be prepared to give an answer to everyone who
asks you to give the reason for the hope that you have."*
1 PETER 3:15

That challenge from St. Peter is not an easy one. Understanding your
Christianity, your beliefs, and your faith is necessary to explain it
to others, and sometimes it is necessary just to maintain one's own faith.
It seems that every point one makes raises more questions. For example,
you might get questions such as: Why are you a Christian? Why should
I believe in Jesus Christ?, What difference does it make?, and on and
on. The questions could be endless. A simple answer could lead to more
questions, such as: So, what? What do you mean Jesus saves?, Saves
from what?, Who was this Jesus Christ?, What do you mean he died
to save me from my sins?, Why would anyone do that or believe that?,
Do you really believe that Jesus died and came back to life?, and so on.
The main purpose of this book is to prepare you to have the answers
for yourself and for others.

It is not enough to be familiar with this subject, or even have a
substantial amount of knowledge about the Bible and Christianity, *the*

1

*level of learning necessary to keep your own faith and to grow as a Christian, and certainly to explain it to others, is **understanding**.*

A. WHY THIS BOOK NOW?

I have been preparing to write this book for some time, but being a great procrastinator, I not only put it off, but also the longer I delayed writing, the more I kept learning more facts that were significant, the more overwhelming the task seemed to become. However, the situation is becoming urgent, so the time has come to set the pen to the paper, and at least present the essentials.

At the time of this "revisit," I am sad to report that the following statistics, which are bad enough, have only gotten worse.

Recent studies are showing that Americans are becoming less Christian and more secular. An *Associated Press* report indicates that while Christianity is still the dominant faith in the United States, only 7 in 10 Americans identify with the tradition. However, the ranks of Christians have declined as the segment of people with no religion has grown. Between 2007 and 2014, Pew research indicates that Americans who describe themselves as atheist, agnostic, or of no particular faith grew from 16 percent to 23 percent. At the same time, Christians dropped from 78 percent to just under 71 percent of the population. The Pew study also found an increase in membership in non-Christian faiths.

Perhaps an even more disturbing trend is that new research is showing that roughly 70 percent of Christian young people who attend church through high school, and while at home, drop away from the faith after they attend a secular college. I must confess that I can relate to this situation, because it happened to me when I left home and entered college in 1949. While I did return to Christianity, stronger than ever, I was absent from almost all church activity and religious learning for roughly twelve years, or until 1961, when I began the road back. Even at that, it was a fairly slow start for the next ten years, or until 1971.

What happens is that young people at that stage begin to have more challenges to their faith and are presented with questions which they are unable to answer. With all the other distractions one has in college, it takes a lot of dedication to get up and to go to church on Sunday morning after having a stay-up-late-good-time on Saturday night. It is just a fact of life, but there are many things that challenge one's faith. There will be professors and peers who will question your faith and challenge you on your beliefs. If you have the opportunity, I urge you to watch a movie entitled *God's Not Dead*. It is available on DVD, and it addresses the issue very well and convincingly.

Despite my personal dark or dim spots, I can say that I never felt that I had abandoned God, nor had He abandoned me. Somehow, I have always had a feeling that He had His hand on my life, and perhaps destiny. One of my favorite hymns is "Amazing Grace," words by John Newton, and one of the verses is especially meaningful to me. It tells us, "Through many dangers, toils and snares, we have already come. Twas grace that led us safe thus far, and grace will lead us home." Indeed, God's grace is sufficient to carry us through our failures, shortcomings, and sins against Him and our fellow man, and all of the tough times.

By the time we finish this book I hope to present convincing evidence that will satisfy one and all that Jesus Christ is for real, He is the son of the one true God, and that the Holy Spirit is also real and acts as God in us. Further, and one of the big questions you will get is: Did Jesus really rise from the dead? You will also be challenged on whether the Bible is true and is it reliable and factual enough to depend upon. With the information in this book, I believe that any reader will be able to stand up and defend Jesus as the Son of God, his resurrection, the Holy Spirit working in us and in our lives and in this world, and in the truth and validity of the Bible. Also, the atheist, agnostic, and humanist will have their eyes opened to God, as the Creator. The totality of the evidence will at least cause the skeptic to realize that there has been some force and control from the beginning of time.

Moral relativism is now the guide for our lives. I used to think that I had a good understanding of "the law." Indeed, I had a decent sense of right and wrong, but now we get legislation on top of more legislation, and it is becoming impossible to be sure of anything. Moral relativism provides no "pole-star," and everything is relative to time and place and the circumstances. It is unable to make moral judgments about what is right or wrong, or to point to any ultimate truth. Who cares about any ethical standards anymore? Corruption is rampant in business and government. Moral relativism leads to the kind of thinking that requires a parent's consent for a child to get an aspirin, but not an abortion. Our Supreme Court can rule that the Ten Commandments may not be displayed in public places, while the Justices sit under such a display in their own court facility.

In America today, what was evil is now becoming something good, and what was right is now wrong. The Bible does provide some absolute truths, and Christians must renew their strength, become aware and concerned, and rethink their positions and take a stand on such issues. For a society to be free and to be workable requires a moral people, who are willing to behave and be obedient to moral laws. Otherwise, we will not have enough police to protect us. We simply cannot afford such immorality. Even for our courts and justice system to work, witnesses must have some fear for lying under oath. Many simply do not care for what the truth might be. Biblical principles provide guidance for individuals and for society.

Our modern society will now contend that there is no such thing as "truth." To this I say, nonsense. Charles Colson writes in his book, *The Faith*:

But our understanding of the universality of the moral law and of our consciences' abilities to understand it has been compromised by today's cultural relativism. This is why many young people, even Christian young people, blanch when I ask them if they believe there are any moral absolutes. But then when I ask them whether it would be right for someone to steal their wallet or to kill someone because they were a Jew or to push an old lady crossing the street into traffic, there is often an "Aha!" moment. Though they have been conditioned to suppress their conscience, educated out of their innate moral sense by postmodern relativism, they instinctively know that those things would never be right.[1]

Colson then contends that even a young child has an innate moral sense which comes to life should another child take his toy. He adds, "The fastest way to provoke scorn from most university professors is to use the words *reality* and *truth*."[2]

The humanist movements, and the so-called sexual revolution, have certainly been forces to challenge our faith and beliefs. We are now confronted with so many abortions. The loss of lives in that way is estimated to be over 55 million (some current estimates put this number as high as 70 million), since the decision in *Roe v. Wade* in 1973 made abortion legal as a way of birth control. We also have the revolution in gay "rights" which is now confronting us in so many ways. The "rights" have most recently been extended to "marriage." I am amazed that such a small minority has been able to create so many new "rights."

Whatever, the aggressiveness of the gay and lesbian movement has been most effective in changing this country. I do not agree with such a lifestyle, and certainly I oppose the idea of gay marriage. (Let them make covenants defining their relationships.) However, in a possible further defense for LGBT sexual activities, I would contend that such is no more a sin than heterosexual fornication and adultery. You be the judge. I will add that we are all sinners in the eyes of God. God loves everyone and wants a relationship with mankind. He offers everyone salvation through belief in Jesus Christ and the sacrifice He made for us. It is a gift and for those who will accept the gift, they (we) are saved only through the grace of God and by belief and faith in Jesus Christ. Christians must also love and be helpful to those who are different, mentally and physically. As a final note on this issue, I would suggest that the gays pray that the Muslims and Islam never win in the world conflict. Sharia law will definitely make some corrections.

The aggressiveness of Muslim groups is also showing growth. They are funded in substantial part by the money they get from the world's purchases of oil. The money is building mosques throughout America, and Arab money is buying access to our education system, and programs selling Islam. It is very noticeable in our Ivy League Universities. Even Duke University agreed to allow the Muslim call to pray on campus, until enough alumni and big financial supporters finally pushed back, and the idea was canceled. How long do you think it would have taken for our politically correct, be tolerant to everyone, judicial system to shut down any attempt for a Christian call for prayer on any public facility? You make the guess.

The militancy of the Muslim Brotherhood and its other affiliated organizations is spread throughout this country and especially on campuses where it is stirring up a vicious rise of anti-Semitism. Time is certainly of the essence to push back and to strengthen and regain our faith as Christians. Christians must not forget that the Jews and Christians worship the same God. The one worshipped by Muslims is definitely not the same. Jesus was a Jew; He is part of the people who made the forever covenant with God, the Father. God has not abandoned the Jews, despite His dispersing of them and periods of punishment for violating their covenant. The Bible makes it clear that the real Jesus of the New Covenant will return and reign with the Jews from Jerusalem. A better understanding of this will be made in chapters concerning the Old and the New Testaments, and The Future.

As bad as things may seem to be, or seem to be getting, there was some encouragement in an article found in *Imprimis*, A Publication of Hillsdale College, April 2015, Volume 44, Number 4. The article was taken from a speech delivered April 21, 2015, at Hillsdale College's Alan P. Kirby Jr. Center for Constitutional Studies and Citizenship by David French, a writer for *National Review*. In his speech, French begins his talk concerning the gay rights battle that was recently held in the state of Indiana and he raises the questions: "Who won the battle of Indiana? Who Lost? What's next for religious Liberty in America?" The article then reads:

> Four truths are emerging: First, the battle is not between gay rights and religious liberty—although religious liberty is certainly at stake—but between the sexual revolution and Christianity itself. This means that Christians are faced not with allegedly "minor" or "insignificant" theological changes to gain leftist acceptance, but with wholesale changes to the historical doctrines of the church.
>
> Second, not a single orthodox denomination is making or even contemplating such changes. This means that tens of millions of Americans will remain—indefinitely—opposed to the continued expansion of the sexual revolution.
>
> Third, rather than going quietly, cultural conservativism is growing in increasing strength at the grassroots—opposing leftist campaigns at the ground level, bypassing politics to support those most embattled by radical hate campaigns.
>
> Fourth, the conservative grassroots and conservative public intellectuals are united . . .

The writer supports the pushbacks by Christians when he cites the failure of the left to boycott Chick-fil-A, the leftist failure against Hobby Lobby, the failure to drive Phil Robertson of Duck Dynasty fame off the television program; and also in Houston, leftist government officials were forced to backtrack after issuing subpoenas requiring area pastors to turn over the contents of their sermons and other communications.

We also must consider what Islam is now doing, the gains that they are making, the atrocities they are committing, and the effect that this is having on the world, but especially throughout the Middle East with the attacks on Christians and non-Muslim believers.

B. WHO IS THIS BOOK FOR?

This book is written for the benefit of everyone: Atheist, Agnostic, Humanist, Hindu, Buddhist, Muslim, Jew, Christian, and especially the marginal Christian who at some time through faith became a believer but fell away with too little understanding to maintain his/her faith whenever challenged. It is hoped that the Agnostic, Atheist, and Humanist will finally believe in God as Creator and Jesus Christ as God in the flesh, and in the Holy Spirit as God in us. It is also hoped that all people will believe in the one true God of Abraham and convert to a belief in Christianity. I realize the difficulty in this, because of the penalties put on any converter from Islam or Hinduism to any other religion, but especially Christianity. However, to the believer in Islam I would ask that they ask themselves: Does the God I believe in love me, is he forgiving, and do I have any hope for salvation? I believe you will find that even the prophet Muhammad admitted that he did not know if he would be in Heaven or Hell, because it would be based upon how much good he did, as opposed to how much evil he had done. Christianity through the saving sacrifice of Jesus Christ does not work that way. Christians can know heaven awaits them if they believe, repent, change direction, and follow the commandments of Jesus. Do not look to get salvation on the "cheap," however.

Overall, I am hoping that what is in this book will help strengthen one's own faith and help the curious to know and understand what Christianity is all about, causing them to become a believer in Jesus

Christ, and to help new believers and seekers to get off to a solid start. For some who have become angry with God or been turned off by the many hard-to-understand events in the Bible it is hoped that this book will provide a turning, or returning, point for them to renew their faith.

Everyone needs to know the hope that Christians have through belief in the saving life and eternal salvation offered by Jesus Christ, which is unique among all religions. This applies to the rich, the poor, the free, the prisoner, the high, the low, and those who think that they have it all, and those who have nothing and feel hopeless. Whatever category you find yourself in, this book is for you. Christianity, above all religions, offers such hope for all eternity. Christians are charged with loving one another and to spread the Gospel of Jesus Christ in order that all may go to Heaven. See, Matthew 28: 19-20 known as the great commission.

Christians are not ordered to kill anyone in order that they might get to Heaven. Christians are to make a friend, be a friend, and bring that friend to Christ.

New Christians, and "sick" Christians need to be fed some spiritual food. While the new "babes" might need mostly "milk," as they begin to mature, they will need some "real" meat. I trust that what you find in this book will provide a "full digestible meal" and be exactly what will meet your needs, wherever you are in this life. In tracking my own background, I am afraid I survived on mostly milk; a faith without real understanding, and a cliché or two for too long. I was already in my forties before I heard the concept of "blood covenants," or anything of real understanding concerning the Holy Spirit. You will know of such things and their significance by the time you finish this book.

I will come to some conclusions that will contradict or conflict with some of the traditions followed by many churches, especially the so-called mainline churches. You can accept the differences or not, as most are not essential to your faith. However, I believe the Bible and the facts support my conclusions, but there are other reasons to

9

support most traditions. For example, we commemorate Jesus's death on "Good Friday." My conclusion is that he actually died on Thursday in the year in which he died. In support of that opinion, I will also support as a fact that Jesus entered Jerusalem on what we refer to as Sunday, "Palm Sunday." I will further support the fact that he was resurrected on what was a Sunday, and for that matter, Easter, the day of Resurrection, will always fall on Sunday according to the Jewish way of celebrating Passover, Unleavened Bread, and the Feast of First Fruits. A more complete explanation will be made of that in the chapter on the New Covenant.

While I strongly believe in these conclusions, it does not matter to me that we commemorate His death on a Friday. What is important is that we remember it and what it means to Christianity. We also celebrate His birth on December 25th, but few people truly believe that He was born on that date, or perhaps even in the cold of winter. What is important is that we celebrate His birth, but most especially His death, burial, and resurrection. Without the resurrection, Christianity is nothing, but I believe the evidence to be presented herein will support the truth of the resurrection of Jesus Christ as the first fruits of the harvest of souls. Prepare your soul for the harvest while there is time.

C. HOW IS THIS BOOK TO BE PRESENTED?

The next chapter will give an overview of the Holy Bible and briefly discuss the significance of the Bible to the world, and its reliability and correctness. Following that we will cover some legal terms and concepts which should help in our understanding of Christianity and the Bible itself. I should mention at this point that I am not a theologian in any way, shape, or form or fashion. While I have made a lengthy study of the Bible and several writers about the Bible, my background is primarily in law and business. I find that many of the terms used in the Bible can help in our understanding when you understand the legal significance of those terms. I am referring to such words as: gifts, covenants, adoption, heir, or so forth.

Following those explanations, we will move into the Old Testament, or Covenant as I prefer to call it, and gain an understanding of covenants, covenant making, and how the Jews were the "covenant people" in their relationship with God. *We must understand the Old Covenant in order to understand the New Covenant, and just how Jesus fulfilled the Old Covenant when making the New Covenant. As Jesus said, "Do not think that I have come to abolish the law or the prophets: I have not come to abolish them, but to fulfill them."* Matthew 5:17. Indeed, he did as you shall see. We must realize that Jesus was born into a Jewish family, was a Jew, and was raised as a Jew. He knew the "law and the prophets." What was in the Old Testament or Covenant was part of His life. We must understand the "law" applicable to Him to understand how He fulfilled it and ushered in the New Covenant as the sacrificial Passover Lamb of God.

As we work through the Old Testament, we will look for things that happened in natural Israel and how they were prophetical for being fulfilled by Jesus, and then how these events and happenings are applicable in the Christian church today. This is a concept I received from listening to tapes on the seven feasts of Israel by Rick Godwin.

We will look at the life and ministry of Jesus Christ and the making of the New Covenant for all humanity. There is no way to cover His life and ministry and all of His teachings and difficult sayings without writing a "library," so the best I will do on those points will be to make a reference to parts of the Bible and mention some good outside sources. I intend to use a few parables to make some needed points about Christianity, what Heaven is like, what God is like, and the difference between the two Kingdoms of Heaven and Earth, but otherwise, I must remain focused, or this work will never end. I finally had to decide that I would have to stick to identifying the essentials and just give references to other things I believe each should know in order to understand the core values and precepts of Christianity.

We cannot complete our understanding of Christianity without understanding how God works in us through the Holy Spirit. Plus, we will need to know how the Holy Spirit was used in the formation of the church and in its growth. Which subject brings us to the question of the Trinity? Some will say that there can only be one God, and to say otherwise is blasphemy.

Rather than devoting much time later to an understanding of the concept of the Holy Trinity, I will try to briefly explain it now. In referring to the Holy Trinity, we are simply looking at God in the three ways He has manifested Himself to us. We have seen Him as creator, as God in the flesh (Jesus Christ), as God in us (the Holy Spirit). God in three persons (one God), blessed Trinity. Consider an automobile. It has an engine to make it move, wheels with a steering mechanism to enable it to move wherever we desire, and a carriage or seat so we can move on it. There are at least these three obvious parts, but one car. Or consider an egg. It has a yolk, with nutrients surrounding it, and an outer shell to hold it all together. There are three parts, but it is one egg. So, where's the problem with the concept of the Holy Trinity?

If we consider God is all powerful, all knowing, all present, or in other words omnipotent, omniscient, omnipresent, where is there a problem with Him being recognizable to mankind in three ways? I hope that is enough said on the issue.

When we think about "the hope we have," we are naturally looking at the future, or the "here-after." Therefore, this book will include a chapter that will consider the future. I am not an expert on eschatology, or the theology of the end times, nor can I predict when or how the end might come, nor have I been given any prophecy on that issue. However, I do have some thoughts based on what is found in the Old and New Testaments, and which have not yet been fulfilled. We are also seeing so many things now that do point toward the promised return of Jesus Christ, the Messiah, and perhaps in the not-too-distant future. It appears that the signs we have been given are becoming more and more apparent and perhaps it is getting to be past time to become prepared, and certainly for ministers of the Gospel to begin informing and warning their parishioners or congregations what is taking place and what might be expected.

Now that you know what this is all about, who it is for, and how this book will develop the understanding you need for your Christian beliefs, we will consider our major source material, the Holy Bible.

CHAPTER 2

THE HOLY BIBLE

*"Blessed is the one who does not walk in step with the
wicked or stand in the way that sinners take or sit in the
company of mockers,*[2] *but whose delight is in the law of the
Lord, and who meditates on his law day and night."*
PSALM 1:1-2

I mentioned in the Dedication how my father was a self-educated Bible
scholar, and he did read, study, and meditate on it, and I thought
enough of him and that issue that I put the citation of Psalm 1:1-2 on
his grave marker. That defined him. He was a truly good man.

The Holy Bible has to be one of the most unique writings ever
assembled. It was written over a period of over fifteen hundred years,
by roughly forty authors, not just one, and in three languages. The
main theme that runs through the Bible moves from creation and the
fall of man to the redemption of man by the new "sacrificial blood"
covenant between the perfect Jesus Christ and God the Father. We are
the undeserving third-party beneficiaries with Jesus as our covenant
head and partner, if we accept His gift and believe. In the next chapter

I will define some of the terms I just used in a more legal and complete sense for your understanding.

The Holy Bible is in two divisions: The Old and the New Covenants, or Testaments. A covenant is synonymous with a contract or agreement, while a testament pertains primarily to wills and takes effect when the maker dies. With those ideas in mind, I look at each half of the Bible more as "covenants." Furthermore, a covenant is more serious and lasting than what we consider as mere contracts in western civilization.

We must always remember, too that the Bible, and especially the Old Testament, was written by Middle Easterners for Middle Easterners and about what was going on in the Middle East, and especially among the Israelites. Whether we are considering the old or the new testaments or covenants, we must not forget the Jewishness of Jesus. If that is a problem for you, you will just have to get over it, because it is a fact.

In the next chapter I will more thoroughly explain or define covenant, how it works, and how they were made by "cutting" a covenant or the shedding of blood.

The Old Covenant contains law, history, poetry, and prophecies of the coming of Jesus and the redemption of all mankind. I must mention that many prophecies pertain to events that have come true. We might *define fulfilled prophesy* as *history before it happens*. Other prophecies are yet to be fulfilled. They give us some foresight of what is to come. Fulfilled prophesy is more evidence of the truth and validity of the Bible.

In the New Covenant we find the fulfillment of the Old Covenant promises and prophecies through the life and sacrifice of Jesus. We also find foresights of things yet to come, or the end of the age. We also learn what God and Heaven are like, and we are more directly introduced to the Holy Spirit.

While there are some points which are difficult to explain, and as people we seem to argue over just about anything, I find that the Bible has withstood the test of time, and is, and can be, generally accepted for what it is. As to some points and conflicts I say, so what? For example, some will question whether Abraham offered Isaac or Ishmael as a sacrifice. The Bible, Christians, and Jews say it was Isaac, but Muslims claim it was Ishmael. I personally believe that it was Isaac, as he was Abraham's son of promise and his true legitimate heir, although not his first born. Whatever, the significance is not about either child, but about Abraham. It was his willingness to obey God, and it was because of that obedience that God trusted Abraham and entered into a covenant with him.

Our sense of logic makes some of the miracles difficult to understand. Perhaps some of the great ones like the exodus from Egypt occurred in a timely manner connected with earthly happenings. If such events were coincidences, I choose to credit them as "God's coincidences." As creator, and I accept it as fact that there was a creator in the development of life on planet Earth, then I can believe that God is capable of anything. He could create, or timely use, such things as storms, earthquakes, tsunamis, or anything to accomplish His will.

The Old Testament is challenged by academia, yet perhaps not as severely as the New Testament when considering Jesus and what He did, and especially His resurrection. I mentioned the Exodus, which except for the resurrection, and now the return of the Jews to their homeland, must be the most significant miracle of all times. We will get into this more when we are studying the Old Testament, but I would like to mention at this time that I was privileged to see a movie titled *Patterns of Evidence.*[1] It did not come to any definite conclusion concerning the Exodus, but it did present the evidence from several points of view and sources. What I concluded from the documentary was that the Exodus did actually happen. There was physical evidence to show that the Israelites were in Egypt, and that there was a mass Exodus at about the time Egypt was essentially destroyed from all of the plagues that were put on it because they refused to let the Israelites leave. It also showed that the area in which they were living was generally undisturbed by these plagues. The homes in that area were more in keeping with what Israelites would have had. There was even a small pyramid-type tomb which was believed to be in honor of Joseph. I was convinced from the documentary that the Exodus did happen, although there was a difference in the evidence in the Egyptian Antiquities challenging who was commonly thought to be the Pharaoh at the time of the Exodus.

The Holy Bible gives us many things. It gives us the law of the Lord. It is a guide for living. It provides for and describes man's relationship with God and the blessings and curses regarding the covenant relationship. If we follow His commands we are blessed, but if we violate the commands, there are curses and penalties to be paid. The Bible makes these quite evident. It gives us examples of God's power.

The Holy Bible is truly a primary foundation of Western thought and wisdom. It is cited in every venue from churches to courts. It was brought to the New World and worked its way into the laws of the United States. It inspired the founders of this country and was used to form the Declaration of Independence and our Constitution, as well as many of our early laws. It is tragic to see how our civilization in the United States of America is being downgraded by humanistic and atheistic thinking and efforts. Our Christian heritage and history are being deconstructed and rewritten to satisfy the ungodly and God haters who seem to have gained a strong foothold in our government, our legal system, academia, and our public education systems. Sadly, and unfortunately, many churches are becoming more and more apostate in order to be more "politically correct." Many churches now fail to stand for, or even show an understanding of what would be "biblically correct."

The Old Testament traces the history of the Jews, Israelites, or Hebrews from the beginning of time to around the middle Fifth Century BC. It begins with the prehistorical subject of the creation and then brings in Abraham and the first major "contract" between God and man. A covenant is earlier mentioned with Noah, that the earth would never again be destroyed by a flood. We are told that the rainbow is a sign of that promise.

The covenant line with Abraham went through Isaac, Abraham's legitimate son, with his wife Sarah. Although it is apparent that Abraham loved his son, Ishmael, who was born of Sarah's servant Hagar, Abraham later sent Ishmael and Hagar away, but with God's promise that he would make through Ishmael a great nation. Isaac, however, was the true "seed" of Abraham and it was the line through Isaac which ultimately led to Jesus. (See Galatians 3:16. See, also, Matthew 1:1-17 for the genealogy of Jesus.)

So long as the Israelites obeyed the requirements of the covenant between God and Abraham and God and Moses, they were blessed, but when they disobeyed, they were punished. Much of the Old Testament gives such history. The blessings could be wonderful, but the curses were harsh, and they affected the whole of Israel, not just the offenders. Much of what God demanded was to protect the Israelites from being corrupted by outside influences with exposure to other gods.

The Old Testament is full of stories. Many of the main characters (Abraham, Moses, and David for example) were shown to be very human, (one might say, "big time sinners"), yet they were forgiven and chosen by God to lead the people. Each one loved God and had a strong relationship with Him. What those stories tell me is that I have a chance for forgiveness, and that God can use anyone willing to obey Him. As we often hear, God does not need our ability, He just needs our availability, our willingness to serve.

The Bible has been challenged by many but has stood the test of time. Although the first five books of the Old Testament are generally credited to Moses, there seems to be no definite agreement on who actually wrote them. No matter who might have written the text, I will accept the Bible in its present form, which is generally agreed to be inspired. I really do not care whose pen was used to produce the writings in the

Old or New Testaments. The same question arises with the Gospels with possible authors mentioned as M, L, and Q. The authorship of the book of Hebrews is also disputed. Many claim it was written by the apostle Paul, but other scholars claim others may have written it. I look more for the "what" rather than for the "who," although "who" can sometimes be significant. In my opinion, adequate authenticity has been established for each book in the Bible.

There are many translations. I am using the New International Version for this work. It conveys the same message, but it just reads a bit easier and clearer than some of the older translations.

The New Testament has also withstood time and tradition, and viewed in the context of its totality, it makes sense. While there are discrepancies between the gospels, most to me are insignificant. For example, the gospel of Mark places the time of Jesus's crucifixion on the day of the Passover, while John places it on the day preceding the Passover. Later I will be using John's version because to me it is more accurate in the totality of the evidence. Some of the confusion or discrepancy might have resulted from the way the Jewish people calculated a day. There will be a more thorough explanation of Jewish calendars and timing in the chapter on the New Covenant.

It is good to look at the New Testament in light of the rules of the evidence. We know that the Gospels were written between thirty-five and sixty-five years after Jesus's death. The Epistles were written closer to the time of Jesus's death. We also know that much of what was written was based on hearsay and passed on from one source to another. So, how can we rely on what has been accepted and included in the New Testament?

There are several ways. We can consider outside sources that had no interest in the subject yet reported what groups of believers were actually doing that tend to corroborate the stories. There are eyewitness reports that were passed on by many. For example, in addition to the disciples, many saw Jesus on several occasions following his death and resurrection. Five hundred or more saw Jesus at one time following his resurrection. Some of the stories about Jesus, and the activities of the New Christian Church started earlier with the letters of Peter, James, John, and Paul. Those letters tend to support what and who Jesus was and what he did and taught. While there might have been a gap between the time of Jesus's death, and the writings in the New Testament, the actual gap for what was consistently observed and later written about was very small, if not nonexistent. The reports were based on what was observed and seen, and talked about contemporaneously with the events, such as the resurrection.

Also, there are exceptions to the rule against hearsay. For example, admissions against interest. There seems to be no dispute that Jesus was crucified, yet for one who was supposedly the Messiah, such a death as a criminal on a cross would have been contrary to what anyone would have thought. Despite his execution as a "criminal," we know that Jesus was buried with honor in a new tomb. Such would be totally out of character for this situation. As the title of one of Josh McDowell's books points out, there is *Evidence That Demands a Verdict*.[2]

Many archeological finds support much of what is in the Old and New Testaments and more such evidence is being discovered all the time. In 1997, Eva and I had the good fortune to visit Israel. Our tour guide was an archeologist, turned tour guide, by the name of Hillel Geva. He edited a book by the title of *Ancient Jerusalem Revealed*.[3] Hillel wrote the first chapter, entitled, "Twenty-Five Years of Excavation in Jerusalem, 1968—1993: Achievements and Evaluations." The revelations, indeed, support much of what is in the Old and the New Testaments.

While the Apostle Paul's first letter or book might have been written twenty years after Jesus's death, what he was reporting concerned things that he had observed and seen during the two years immediately after Jesus's death and the beginning of the Church. At that time, Saul (later Paul) was persecuting the Christians, and he saw and observed all that they were doing and saying. Most of what went on even in this period and especially in the Old Testament was verbal by word of mouth and passed on. While we all know what can happen to stories that get passed on in our little game, here the same stories were observed and retold by many. The core theology developed, and it can be taken more as truth and factual.

For a brief but excellent explanation concerning the validity and truthfulness of the Bible and especially the New Testament, and something that would help people to maintain their faith in light of skepticism and criticism from academia, I suggest the reading of a booklet based on a conversation between Dr. John Ankerberg and Dr. Darrell Bock. The title is *Questions the World Will Ask about Your Faith*. It was published in 2015 by ATRI Publishing of Chattanooga, Tennessee. Dr. John Ankerberg is the founder of the Ankerberg Theological Research Institute, and Dr. Darrell Bock is senior Research Professor of New Testament Studies at Dallas Theological Seminary.

It appears to me that the validity and truthfulness of the Bible, whether for the Old or New Testament, is far more valid than many other writings of history, and especially those that did not get reported in writing until hundreds of years after a certain event happened. If one can believe such stories, one can certainly believe what is found in the Bible. When we consider the whole theme, how it was authored by forty individuals in three languages over a long period of time, it makes one feel as if the information was provided to the writers by some outside divine source. The totality of the Bible is such that it simply could not have been made up.

The story of the resurrection must be the most significant one in the Bible because without the resurrection, Christianity would have little more to offer than most other religions. This will be covered later in this book, but for now let's touch briefly on the evidence of the resurrection. The Bible offers reports of Jesus being seen by many and various groups following his resurrection. In one case, he was seen by more than five hundred witnesses. This number would only include the men.

As a lawyer or judge that would be sufficient evidence, but, more important, let's look at the creditability of the witnesses. In the case of the disciples who surely saw him and were with him following the resurrection, they told the story in various parts of the world. Most were executed and some tortured, but not one recanted the story of having known and seen the resurrected Jesus. It is conceivable that one might die for a lie, truly believing the story to be true, but I cannot imagine anyone dying as the disciples did knowing that something was a lie. They knew the truth, and professed it to their dying breaths, comparable to a dying declaration (another exception to the rule against hearsay).

An example of evidence from an outside source supporting the Exodus from Egypt was given by Rahab to the spies sent into Jericho before the Israelites entered to take the city and the land. In Joshua 2:8-11, we find:

> [8]Before the spies lay down for the night, she went up on the roof [9]and said to them, "I know that the Lord has given you this land and that a great fear of you has fallen on us, so that all who live in this country are melting in fear because of you. [10]*We have heard how the Lord dried up the water of the Red Sea for you when you came out of Egypt,* and what you did to Sihon and Og, the two kings of the Amorites east of the Jordan, whom you completely destroyed. [11]When we heard of it, our hearts melted in fear and everyone's courage failed because of you, for the Lord your God is God in heaven above and on the earth below. (Emphasis added)

The people throughout the Middle East knew of the Exodus and what God had done for the Israelites during the forty years before finally entering their Promised Land.

23

I will not spend more time giving my own support for the Bible, other than to say that I accept it. It has been scrutinized and critically examined by many experts and scholars and it is generally accepted. I believe what I will be using to support my understanding of the Bible and Christianity is true and accurate. None of us were there, and we must rely on what we have been given. In my opinion, the proponents of the Bible have met their burden of "truth-proof." As to the points in the Bible that I will be using, the burden of any repudiation should fall on the skeptics.

When Jesus was talking to His doubting apostle Thomas, we learn: "Because you have seen me, you have believed; blessed are those who have not seen and yet have believed." John 20: 29. That is where we are. We were not there to see the risen Christ and must, therefore, believe by faith. Our faith, however, is affirmed and confirmed by the totality of the evidence.

The Holy Bible is undoubtedly one of the most important books in developing the wisdom of the West. It is the greatest book ever written, the most sold and widely distributed book ever published, and it contains the greatest story ever told about the greatest life ever lived.

In considering what the Bible has to offer us, I will be looking for the context in the times in which it was written. For example, the Bible is written about and by people of the Middle East and involves a culture very unlike our culture of today, especially those living outside of the Middle East. In Bible times most of the people had little or no formal education. They were mostly agrarian and nomadic people. They were sheep keepers and knew all about the characteristics of sheep and such animals, so many of stories and illustrations relate to what they knew, did, and understood. If you know something about the nature of sheep and their relationship to the shepherd, you can more clearly understand the 23rd Psalm.

People of the Bible made covenants and sacrifices which will be discussed in more detail later. We in the Western culture make contracts and then begin looking for ways to break them. Covenants in Middle

Eastern context, were, and are, lasting agreements and carried on from generation to generation. They contain promises and responsibilities, and blessings and curses for keeping and breaking the agreement. Although blood covenants are still made in some cultures today perhaps the closest thing we experience to covenants in our society is the covenant of marriage. However, some of the older readers might remember "cowboy movies" where the Indian and the White man would make a covenant by cutting their wrist and letting the blood flow together. They became "blood brothers" and "covenant partners" with one another. How our Native Americans ever conceived this idea and method of making a blood covenant, I simply do not know.

God would be dealing with people in ways they would understand. Likewise, the people would deal with one another in ways they could understand.

What the Bible primarily traces for us from the time man was expelled from Eden is the relationship between God and man to reconnect and return to paradise.

The final point of redemption comes with the establishment of the New Covenant through the atoning power of the blood sacrifice of Jesus Christ, as the one and only perfect Lamb of God. Hopefully this point will be perfectly clear by the time we finish covering the New Covenant in chapter 5.

These contextual points should help with conceptual understandings of many points in the Bible and in the explanation of my understanding of Christianity.

As somewhat of a postscript, I would like to mention that I have reviewed a book by the title of *As a Lawyer Sees Jesus* [4] written by Judge Clarence Bartlett (incidentally another Kentucky Judge, this one from Owensboro). I found this book to be an excellent support for the authenticity of the Bible based on many applicable rules of evidence. I refer all skeptics to this book.

Christians tend to argue over any and everything and split off into various denominations and beliefs. Some differences are significant to the point of affecting the essentials of what Christians believe or should believe. Some are disturbing to the point that it is hard to understand where in the Bible such ideas are coming from. I will not single out any at this time, but some may come to light as we progress through this book. However, many of the differences are inconsequential, but nevertheless can cause nonbelievers to wonder just what Christianity is all about.

With so many denominations, the nonbeliever can really get confused. For example, I recall my time in Japan in 1954-55. There were at least three missionaries from three denominations in my area. I would get questions about Christianity, and what were the differences. Unfortunately, at that time I could not give any clear answer, otherwise some lives might have been changed.

Some differences pertain to governance such as hierarchal or congregational, others might involve the type of worship service, such as liturgical or praise and preaching. None of these differences should detract from the basic belief that Jesus Christ is the son of God who came into the world to save all sinners. You and I fall into that category.

I do not wish to make light of the problem of biblical interpretations, but I heard a joke a few years ago which clearly illustrates just how silly some differences might be. As the story goes, a man was driving through the Bible Belt and stopped for gas. While pumping, he looked across the street and saw two almost identical buildings which appeared to be churches. The sign on one read: Goodwill, Freewill, Two Peas in the Pod Church. The other read: Goodwill, Freewill, Two Peas in the Pod *Reformed* Church. So, while scratching his head in wonder, he asked the attendant if he could tell him the difference in the two. The attendant replied, "Oh, yes, the regular church believes that Pharaoh's daughter found Moses in the bulrushes, but those at the reformed church believe that Pharaoh's daughter *says* she found Moses in the bulrushes." Go figure.

Skeptics will forever attempt to challenge the truth and validity of the Bible. Some simply do not want to believe the content, nor the message, and they will pick and choose any item of disagreement to make their case. Such foes might look inwardly to discover their own lack of understanding of what Christianity is all about and the totality of the overall message. For the ones refusing to believe, reasons to continue to disbelieve can continue to be found, but for the one looking for truth and ultimate salvation through the atoning blood sacrifice of Jesus Christ, there is solid evidence to stand on. We can all use some faith and trust, as well as knowledge and understanding. I believe this book together with the Bible will help the reader reach such goals.

Before moving into the Old Testament or covenant, we will next consider legal terms and definitions that should help in understanding what Christianity is all about and how it works. We will more specifically look at covenant making and blood covenants.

†

CHAPTER 3

LEGAL TERMS TO HELP IN YOUR UNDERSTANDING

"For it is by grace you have been saved, through faith—
and this is not from yourselves, it is the gift of God."
EPHESIANS 2:8

The word "gift" appears in many places in the Bible, and it is important to know what a gift is and how it works. In the legal sense a gift requires a donor with donative or giving intent of something of value and a recipient who accepts it. In other words, if I say, "I give you my watch" and hand it to you, it is not a completed gift. You must accept it to complete it. The same applies with this gift from God. It is nothing if you do not accept it. Some other examples we find using the word gift would involve the gift of eternal life in Jesus Christ as we find in Romans 6:23, "For the wages of sin is death, but the gift of God is eternal life in Christ Jesus our Lord."

All humans are sinners. The result of sin is eternal death. But through the atoning death and sacrifice of Jesus Christ in the covenant

He made with God the Father for our benefit, we can have eternal life, if we believe, repent, change our ways, and follow His commandments. I will mention also that we have gifts of the Holy Spirit. They are found in 1 Corinthians, Chapter 12. These gifts may be just given and accepted and used because they are just there. However, they may also come as a result of a request that you make. Nevertheless, whether they are freely given, or come after a request, they still must be accepted.

By comparison we are also told that there is fruit of the Spirit. These are identified and enumerated in various places, but we specifically find several in Galatians 5:22 and 23, which reads: "²²But the fruit of the Spirit is love, joy, peace, forbearance, kindness, goodness, faithfulness, ²³gentleness and self-control. Against such things there is no law."

We can draw a distinction between gifts and fruit in this sense. A gift is something that is immediate, but something identified as fruit must grow and develop into maturity and ripeness. You can see by the nature of these fruits of the Spirit that they are characteristics which have to be developed over time. Human nature just doesn't give them to us immediately. The word gift does appear throughout the Bible in many places, but as you read that word, keep in mind it is nothing for your benefit, unless you accept it. I urge you to do it!

Another term that is quite significant is the word "heir." In Galatians 3:29 we learn: "If you belong to Christ, then you are Abraham's seed, and heirs according to the promise." We also see in Galatians 4:7: "So you are no longer a slave, but God's child; and since you are his child, God has made you also an heir." For one more, consider Romans 8:17 which reads, "Now if we are children, then we are heirs—heirs of God and co-heirs with Christ, if indeed we share in his sufferings in order that we may also share in his glory."

In a legal sense, an heir is one that inherits from a parent or family member. We find the word "inherit" in various places in the Bible, but for example in Matthew 25:34 we find: "Then the King will say to those on his right come you who are blessed by my Father take your inheritance the kingdom prepared for you since the creation of the world." We should note that being an heir and having an inheritance applies to Gentiles as well as Jews. Paul writes in Ephesians 3:6: "⁶This mystery is that through the gospel the Gentiles are heirs together with Israel, members together of one body, and sharers together in the promise in Christ Jesus." Just imagine being a coheir in God's Kingdom with Jesus Christ.

You may wonder how we become heirs, sons, and coheirs with Jesus Christ. We are told that it is by "adoption." That word also appears in several places. Ephesians 1:5, provides: "⁵He predestined us for adoption to sonship through Jesus Christ, in accordance with his pleasure and will—." In a legal sense, adoption refers to the taking or receiving as one's own that to which he had no prior relation. Further, an adopted child inherits just as a natural child.

In many translations of the Bible, we find that Jesus Christ is our "mediator and advocate." In 1 John 2:1-2, we can know: "¹My dear children, I write this to you so that you will not sin. But if anybody does sin, we have an advocate with the Father—Jesus Christ, the Righteous One. ²He is the atoning sacrifice for our sins, and not only for ours but also for the sins of the whole world." What this tells us is that Christ is our attorney. On judgment day, He may be a prosecutor or our defender, but my prediction is that He has never lost a case, and never will. May your and my name be in His Book. You may think you know Him, but does He know you? It is my prayer that on that day, as I stand before God with my head bowed in shame, the charges are read, and I know that I am guilty AS sin, of innumerable sins, Jesus will step forward and announce that I am one of His, and that He has already paid my penalty. Case dismissed. Praise God and Jesus!

Two other terms I will use from time to time will be "beneficiary" and "third-party beneficiary." While neither is found in the Bible, they are nevertheless appropriate. An heir who receives something is a beneficiary. A beneficiary receives something of value, whether a right, property, or advantage. A third-party beneficiary is one who receives a benefit from an agreement, a contract, or covenant made by others to which he was not a party. However, it must appear that the contract was actually made for his benefit. This is precisely the situation where Jesus Christ made a Covenant with God the Father by sacrificing and shedding His own blood which was to atone for the sins of mankind. We are all the undeserving third-party beneficiaries of that New Covenant, if we believe in Jesus Christ as our savior, and receive and accept His gift. We must also confess to Him that we are sinners and repent of our sins, convert and change our ways, and obey His commandments.

Concerning the concepts of mediator, inheritance, testament, will, death, and blood, I will add one more biblical citation—Hebrews 9:15-18.

> [15] *For this reason Christ is the mediator of a new covenant, that those who are called may receive the promised eternal inheritance—now that he has died as a ransom to set them free from the sins committed under the first covenant.* [16] *In the case of a will, it is necessary to prove the death of the one who made it,* [17] *because a will is in force only when somebody has died; it never takes effect while the one who made it is living.* [18] *This is why even the first covenant was not put into effect without blood.* (Emphasis added)

Give some second and third thoughts to this passage.

In *Strong's Exhaustive Concordance of the Bible*, the word "testament" appears a few times, while the word "covenant" appears a few hundred times. Obviously, the concept of covenant is significant. In law, the term testament applies to wills. Property is to be distributed, but only after the death of the testator. The term certainly has an application to the Bible and the relationships therein, but the term covenant is, to me, overall, more appropriate. The remainder of this chapter will concentrate on defining the terms covenant and especially explaining the concept of a blood covenant.

In our western culture, we generally think in terms of contracts, and once made, how to enforce them or get out of them. The essential elements are an agreement and an obligation with sufficient consideration, with payment, or a promise to do something. If everything is done, a contract is "executed." If something remains to be done, it is "executory." Contracts may be written or oral, with some evidence to make them enforceable. Textbooks and thousands of cases have been written about all types of contracts, but perhaps this is enough said for these purposes.

A "covenant" is a contract, but more formal. In Western law we see them more generally in deeds or land titles. They are intended to be lasting and provide warranties.

Vines Complete Expository Dictionary of Old and New Testament Words defines "Covenant" as "A. Noun. Primarily signifies a disposition of property by will or otherwise. It is a rendering of a Hebrew word meaning a 'covenant' or agreement (from a verb signifying *'to cut or divide,' in an allusion to a sacrificial custom in connection with 'covenant making,'* . . . ." (Emphasis added)

Covenant makers in the Bible would come together and present to the other party, their coats, armor, belts, and such, signifying that they were giving the other party all of themselves and their strength. If one ever needed something or some help, the partner had pledged to be there. The Hebrew people would often sacrifice (cut, divide) an animal, lay it out in two parts and walk through the parts in a figure 8. Bloodshed would be part of the covenant making. They would define the blessings and curses: (i.e., what good you get for keeping the covenant, and what you are going to "get," if you violate the terms.) (For the blessings and the curses between God and the Israelites, see generally: Deuteronomy Chapters 6, 7 & 8.) In some cases, there would be a name change. Usually, there would also be a memorial. It could be a meal, a pile of rocks, or the planting of a tree or shrub. The covenant meal for the covenant between God and Abraham was not prescribed and ordained until the time of the Passover, over four hundred years later.

Since the terms and conditions would be ongoing, these would not only be lasting and generational, but would be executory, until terminated for some reason, or by agreement.

Perhaps marriage is the closest example of living in covenant which we have today. However, even marriage has almost been decimated by our modern laws. It was meant to create families and be lasting for generations. Where it was next to impossible to get a divorce, for the past sixty years or so in most American States, all that is now required is for one of the parties to say that the marriage is irretrievably broken.

There are many covenants in the Bible. Some are between man and man (we will look at the covenant between David and Jonathan), and some between God and man. We will primarily look at the covenant between God and Abram (later changed to Abra*ha*m), and between Jesus and God. These are the two that provide the foundation for the Old Testament (or Covenant) and the New Testament (or Covenant). However, we will also refer to the covenants between Moses and God and David and God, but will not be involved with other covenants, such as between God and Noah.

We will next begin our overview of the Old Covenant, which must be understood to understand the New Covenant, and how Jesus fulfilled the law and the prophecies of the Old Testament.

✝

CHAPTER 4

THE OLD TESTAMENT-COVENANT

"¹In the beginning God created the heavens and the earth."
GENESIS 1:1

A. IN THE BEGINNING

You might wonder why I begin this chapter with that passage. I have several reasons. First, this is how the Old Testament begins. However, and more important, it tells us that God created the heavens and the earth. If you do not believe in God the Creator, there is no way you will ever believe in Jesus Christ, and if you do not believe in Jesus Christ, you will never be a Christian, nor will your soul be eligible for eternity with God.

This passage will create difficulties for atheists, agnostics, humanists, and any others who merely believe that the earth and all life merely happened by accident and evolved over billions of years. It is my hope that when nonbelievers, and believers who have been taught nothing but that the "theory" of evolution is "scientific fact," read this book, they will see the connections throughout recorded history between mankind and a Creator who is still in charge. You can then believe with some certainty that the earth was created by God from the beginning.

It should be noted on this "revisit" that since the book was first published in 2015, science has found that the universe did have a beginning. In physical cosmology, the age of the universe since the "big bang" has been calculated to be almost fourteen billion years. Some estimates conclude a shorter time, but nevertheless a beginning. More information on this issue can be found in *Wikipedia*. If the universe began with a big bang, who or what created it? Modern scientific discoveries and evidence, together with historical facts and evidence and personal experiences are making it more and more difficult to deny the existence of God as creator.

Ask yourself a few questions. If there is no God, what is the meaning of life? What is life's value or purpose, or is it all an illusion? If God is dead, is man not also dead? What is the hope for humanity? Are we just playing some game trying to do, or amount to, something? Who has or can explain how life came from nonlife? No one has done that yet. Where did we get our sense of ought or morality? Even Charles Darwin had doubts about his theory of evolution and natural selection. Fossils from the Cambrian era indicate an explosion of new life forms with no explanation for their origins.

Life is so complex that I just cannot believe I could go to a local junkyard that had every type of thing in it; stick several pieces of dynamite underneath the pile; blow it up, and then have it all fall into place in the form of a Boeing 747 aircraft ready for takeoff. That would never happen no matter how many times I tried to recreate the situation by blowing up a junkyard. It is even more difficult for me to believe that all the complicated life forms somehow evolved from microscopic ooze.

Human life is extremely complex. Try to explain, if you will, or can, where did we get our sexuality and X and Y chromosomes? How about our DNA? If you cannot answer these questions, then I challenge you to at least open your mind to the possibility, no, the reality, that there is a God as creator, and at least the intelligent designer.

My engineer son has explained to me that in the creation of things there are five elements. There is time, a force, action, space, and matter. If you reread Genesis 1:1 you will find each of those five elements in order. In the beginning (time), God (force), created (action), the heavens (space), and the earth (matter).

I also find it interesting that in the remainder of Genesis Chapter 1 we are given the sequence in which things were created beginning on the first day with light and concluding the sixth day with man. In verse 27, we read, "So God created mankind in his own image, in the image of God he created them; male and female he created them." Genesis 1:27. At the end of the "sixth day" the heavens and earth were completed, so on the seventh day God rested.

I have no idea how long each of these "days" might have been, and personally for me it does not matter whether it was a 24-hour day or an eon. The bottom line is that there was a creator whom we refer to as God. We might note at this time, however, that the basis for the Jewish day comes from these passages where they refer to "and there was evening, and there was morning—the first day." They begin the day at sundown and have a night half that lasts until sunrise and a day half which goes from sunrise to sunset. Morning follows the evening. This will be discussed more thoroughly as we consider in the New Testament the way the Jews calculate a day, their year, and their religious and civil calendars.

Next comes the story of Adam and Eve, and I do not wish to get bogged down with all the debate that might ensue on that subject. However, it does teach me several lessons. Man could live in perfect harmony with nature and God by obeying God, but they disobeyed and allowed the evil one, the fallen angel Lucifer, or the Devil, to entice them to eat the forbidden fruit. They were trying to become like gods themselves and know everything. Adam and Eve were then removed from this perfect paradise and thereafter had to suffer the consequences. Sin came into the world, they had Cain and Abel, and over jealousy, Cain killed Abel. Cain was sent off to the East of Eden. Adam and Eve had other children which then began to help populate the world. But again, and prior to God giving the law, the world became corrupted to the point that God was ready to destroy mankind and start over with someone who would be trustworthy. God chose Noah.

From the fall of man, God has been attempting to reconnect with mankind, and bring him/her back to paradise.

Noah had three sons with families and they along with pairs of animals were saved when the world was flooded. The three families begin to repopulate the world. Noah's sons were Shem, Ham, and Japheth. Shem's family became known as Semites. And thus begins the redemption of mankind by God through the call to Abram, who was a descendent of Shem.

Already I have gone outside what is needed for explaining the parts of the Old Testament or Covenant necessary to understand the New Testament or Covenant. While there are many interesting stories in the Bible, and I encourage you to read them for yourself, I will break the remainder of this chapter into several subsections. The first will be the making of the Covenant with Abram (Abraham) and the development of the twelve tribes of Israel. The next sections will cover the journey into Egypt and the Exodus. The third area will be the giving of the law(s), and finally, we will look at many of the prophecies pertaining to the coming of Jesus.

B. THE ABRAHAMIC COVENANT

In Genesis 12:1-3 we find the call to Abram:

> The Lord had said to Abram, Go from your country, your people and your father's household to the land I will show you. ²I will

make you into a great nation, and I will bless you; I will make your name great, and you will be a blessing. *³I will bless those who bless you, and whoever curses you I will curse; and all peoples on earth will be blessed through you.* (Emphasis add)

Anyone cursing Israel today should read the foregoing passage carefully!! Pay attention!! Stop picking on the Jews!! (Thus saith the Lord!!!)

At this time Abram was seventy-five-years old. We will soon note that the complete making of this covenant will take roughly twenty-five years.

Abram responded to the call and moved with his wife, Sarai, his nephew Lot and all of their possessions, into the land of Canaan. Abram and Lot finally separated, and Abram stayed in Canaan and Lot moved southeast into the area near Sodom.

When Abram was approximately ninety years old, we find in Genesis 15:1-18, the following:

After this, the word of the Lord came to Abram in a vision: "Do not be afraid, Abram. I am your shield, your very great reward." ²But Abram said, "Sovereign Lord, what can you give me since I remain childless and the one who will inherit my estate is Eliezer of Damascus?" ³And Abram said, "You have given me no children; so a servant in my household will be my heir." ⁴Then the word of the Lord came to him: "This man will not be your heir, *but a son who is your own flesh and blood will be your heir.*" ⁵He took him outside and said, *"Look up at the sky and count the stars—if indeed you can count them." Then he said to him, "So shall your offspring be."* ⁶Abram believed the Lord, and he credited it to him as righteousness. ⁷He also said to him, "I am the Lord, who brought you out of Ur of the Chaldeans to give you this land to take possession of it." *⁸But Abram said, "Sovereign Lord, how can I know that I will gain possession of it?"*

It is at this point that they actually begin *cutting* and making the covenant.

> *9 So the Lord said to him, "Bring me a heifer, a goat and a ram, each three years old, along with a dove and a young pigeon."* 10 Abram brought all these to him, *cut them in two and arranged the halves opposite each other; the birds, however, he did not cut in half.* 11 Then birds of prey came down on the carcasses, but Abram drove them away. 12 As the sun was setting, Abram fell into a deep sleep, and a thick and dreadful darkness came over him. 13 Then the Lord said to him, *"Know for certain that for four hundred years your descendants will be strangers in a country not their own and that they will be enslaved and mistreated there."*

This was the foretelling of the time the Israelites would be in captivity in Egypt, much of it as slaves. The covenant meal as a lasting requirement was prescribed at the time of the Israelites delivery from their captivity in Egypt.

> "14 But I will punish the nation they serve as slaves, and *afterward they will come out with great possessions.* 15 You, however, will go to your ancestors in peace and be buried at a good old age. 16 In the fourth generation your descendants will come back here, for the sin of the Amorites has not yet reached its full measure. 17 *When the sun had set and darkness had fallen, a smoking firepot with a blazing torch appeared and passed between the pieces.* 18 *On that day the Lord made a covenant with Abram and said, "To your descendants I give this land, from the Wadi of Egypt to the great river, the Euphrates."* (Emphasis added)

Here we have a description of the "Promised Land."

Sarai had given Abram no children and was barren and in old age. However, she had an Egyptian maid servant named Hagar and Sarai give her to Abram through which to have a son. From this union Ishmael was born. Ishmael was Abram's first born, but he was not to become his heir.

The final making of the Covenant and its completion came when Abram was ninety-nine-years old. This continuation and completion required circumcision which involved blood from Abram and those entering the Covenant and it was at this time that the names and Abram and Sarai were changed to Abra*ha*m and Sara*h*. God's name was somewhat of an unpronounceable "H" or "Ha" sound. That letter and sound was put in as part of the name of each. This is one of the points I remember from the Malcolm Smith tapes.

In Genesis Chapter 17:1-16, we are taught:

¹When Abram was *ninety-nine years old*, the Lord appeared to him and said, "I am God Almighty; walk before me faithfully and be blameless. ²Then *I will make my covenant between me and you and will greatly increase your numbers.*" ³Abram fell facedown, and God said to him, ⁴"As for me, this is my covenant with you: You will be the father of many nations. ⁵*No longer will you be called Abram; your name will be Abraham*, for I have made you a father of many nations. ⁶I will make you very fruitful; I will make nations of you, and kings will come from you. ⁷*I will establish my covenant as an everlasting covenant between me and you and your descendants after you for the generations to come, to be your God and the God of your descendants after you.* ⁸The whole land of Canaan, where you now reside as a foreigner, I will give as an everlasting possession to you and your descendants after you; and I will be their God." ⁹Then God said to Abraham, "*As for you, you must keep my covenant, you and your descendants after you for the generations to come.* ¹⁰This is my covenant with you and your descendants

41

after you, the covenant you are to keep: *Every male among you shall be circumcised.* [11] *You are to undergo circumcision, and it will be the sign of the covenant between me and you.* [12] *For the generations to come every male among you who is eight days old must be circumcised, including those born in your household or bought with money from a foreigner—those who are not your offspring.* [13]Whether born in your household or bought with your money, they must be circumcised. My covenant in your flesh is to be an everlasting covenant. [14]Any uncircumcised male, who has not been circumcised in the flesh, will be cut off from his people; he has broken my covenant." [15]*God also said to Abraham, "As for Sarai your wife, you are no longer to call her Sarai; her name will be Sarah.* [16]*I will bless her and will surely give you a son by her.* I will bless her so that she will be the mother of nations; kings of peoples will come from her." (Emphasis added for special attention)

The Covenant is now complete, Isaac has been promised, and Abraham is informed that the Covenant will run through him. The birth of Isaac appears in Genesis 21 and Abraham is now one hundred and Sarah is ninety. Abraham is the "covenant head" which is to run eternally for generations to come through Isaac and Jacob and, ultimately, Jesus.

Ishmael was probably about eight years older than Isaac, and when Isaac was still very young and perhaps Ishmael around ten, or maybe twelve, Sarah observed Ishmael mocking Isaac and insisted to Abraham that he have Hagar and Ishmael leave. Abraham was very distressed by this, but he did send both away with his blessing for Ishmael and God's promise that he would make of Ishmael a great nation. We are told that Ishmael became an archer, lived in the desert, and that Hagar found an Egyptian wife for him. Despite this division between Isaac and Ishmael, it is interesting to note that when Abraham died both sons came together to bury him. We know this from Genesis 25:9-10:

⁹His sons Isaac and Ishmael buried him in the cave of Machpelah near Mamre, in the field of Ephron son of Zohar the Hittite, ¹⁰the field Abraham had bought from the Hittites. There Abraham was buried with his wife Sarah.

Referring back to the time when Isaac was a child, God tested Abraham one more time. The story of Abraham's willingness to sacrifice Isaac can be found in Genesis 22:1-14. We know that at the last minute a ram trapped in a thicket was provided and used as the sacrifice and Isaac was released. God's pleasure with Abraham is found in verses 15-18 which read:

"¹⁵The angel of the Lord called to Abraham from heaven a second time ¹⁶and said, "I swear by myself, declares the Lord, that because you have done this and have not withheld your son, your only son, ¹⁷I will surely bless you and make your descendants as numerous as the stars in the sky and as the sand on the seashore. Your descendants will take possession of the cities of their enemies, ¹⁸and through your offspring all nations on earth will be blessed, because you have obeyed me."

Abraham sent Isaac back to the country of their people in the area of Ur. There Isaac found Rebecca, who was the granddaughter of Nahor the brother of Abraham. Isaac and Rebecca had two sons Esau and Jacob. While they were perhaps maternal twins Esau was the first born and Jacob followed. They were very different. In Isaac's old age Rebecca and Jacob tricked Isaac into giving Jacob the blessing rather than Esau. The line and covenant ran through Jacob.

Jacob had twelve sons born of his wives Leah and Rachel, and two maids one of Leah and one of Rachel. Leah bore the first four sons for Jacob. They were Rubin, Simeon, Levi, and Judah. The line from Abraham through Isaac and Jacob and David and on to Jesus went through Judah. The fifth and sixth sons were borne by Bilhah, the maid servant of Rachel. Their names were Dan and Naphtali. Leah had stopped having children and gave her maid servant Zilpah to Jacob and she bore Gad and Asher. Leah was later able to conceive, and she gave a fifth and sixth son to Jacob by the names Issachar and Zebulun. Leah was also the mother of at least one daughter, named Dinah. Rachel had been unable to conceive but finally she became pregnant and gave birth to Joseph, and later to Benjamin.

To better understand how a covenant with Abraham passed on for the benefit of not only the Jew, but also the Gentiles, we need to look at the explanation by the Apostle Paul in his letter to the Galatians. We need to consider most of the passages in chapter 3. Galatians 3:6-19, provides:

"[6]So also Abraham "believed God, and it was credited to him as righteousness." [7]Understand, then, that *those who have faith are children of Abraham.* [8]Scripture foresaw that *God would justify the Gentiles by faith* and *announced the gospel in advance to Abraham: "All nations will be blessed through you."* [9]So those who rely on faith are blessed along with Abraham, the man of faith.

The explanation continues in verses 14-18:

[14]He redeemed us in order that *the blessing given to Abraham might come to the Gentiles through Christ Jesus, so that by faith we might receive the promise of the Spirit.*

[15]Brothers and sisters, let me take an example from everyday life. *Just as no one can set aside or add to a human covenant that*

has been duly established, so it is in this case. [16]*The promises were spoken to Abraham and to his seed. Scripture does not say "and to seeds," meaning many people, but "and to your seed," meaning one person, who is Christ.* [17]*What I mean is this: The law, introduced 430 years later, does not set aside the covenant previously established by God and thus do away with the promise.* [18]For if the inheritance depends on the law, then it no longer depends on the promise; but God in his grace gave it to Abraham through a promise. (Emphasis added)

We know that Abraham made a covenant with God which would be lasting forever, and as Paul points out, even to benefit the Gentiles. Abraham was the "covenant head" which covered those of us (Jew, Gentile, and all) who have come along afterward.

C. THE COVENANT BETWEEN DAVID AND JONATHAN

Another example of covenant making which clearly shows how covenants are to last from generation to generation is the covenant between David and Jonathan (King Saul's son). In this illustration of a covenant between men, each party would be a covenant head for their children and heirs. We find the making of this covenant in 1 Samuel 18:3-4. "[3]And Jonathan made a covenant with David because he loved him as himself. [4]Jonathan took off the robe he was wearing and gave it to David, along with his tunic, and even his sword, his bow and his belt."

I would assume that David did the same thing. They pledged all their strength and everything they had to each other in the event the other might need it.

King Saul became very distrustful of David and angry with him. On several occasions he attempted to kill David. However, Jonathan came forward to prevent that and was able to save David's life.

In a later battle, both Jonathan and Saul were killed, and David became king. In those days children or relatives of former kings were certainly subject to being disposed of and eliminated as a threat to the new king. In 2 Samuel Chapter 9 we find just how this covenant lived on. In verses 1-13, we read:

David asked, "Is there anyone still left of the house of Saul to whom I can show kindness for Jonathan's sake?" ²Now there was a servant of Saul's household named Ziba. They summoned him to appear before David, and the king said to him, "Are you Ziba?" "At your service," he replied. ³The king asked, "Is there no one still alive from the house of Saul to whom I can show God's kindness?" Ziba answered the king, "There is still a son of Jonathan; he is lame in both feet." ⁴"Where is he?" the king asked. Ziba answered, "He is at the house of Makir son of Ammiel in Lo Debar." ⁵So King David had him brought from Lo Debar, from the house of Makir son of Ammiel. ⁶When Mephibosheth son of Jonathan, the son of Saul, came to David, he bowed down to pay him honor. David said, "Mephibosheth!" "At your service," he replied. ⁷"Don't be afraid," David said to him, "for I will surely show you kindness for the sake of your father Jonathan. I will restore to you all the land that belonged to your grandfather Saul, and you will always eat at my table." ⁸Mephibosheth bowed down and said, "What is your servant, that you should notice a dead dog like me?" ⁹Then the king summoned Ziba, Saul's steward, and said to him, "I have given your master's grandson everything that belonged to Saul and his family. ¹⁰You and your sons and your servants are to farm the land for him and bring in the crops, so that your master's grandson may be provided for. And Mephibosheth, grandson of your master, will always eat at my table." (Now Ziba had fifteen sons and twenty servants.) ¹¹Then Ziba said to the king, "Your servant will do whatever my lord the king commands his servant to do." So Mephibosheth ate at David's table like one of the king's sons. ¹²Mephibosheth had a young son named Mika, and all the members of Ziba's household were servants of Mephibosheth. ¹³And Mephibosheth lived in Jerusalem, because he always ate at the king's table; he was lame in both feet.

The story of David and Jonathan provides an excellent example of how the heirs of a "covenant partner" are supposed to benefit.

D. THE MOVE INTO EGYPT

¹These are the names of the sons of Israel who went to Egypt with Jacob, each with his family: ²Reuben, Simeon, Levi and Judah; ³Issachar, Zebulun and Benjamin; ⁴Dan and Naphtali; Gad and Asher. ⁵The descendants of Jacob numbered seventy in all; Joseph was already in Egypt. (Exodus 1:1-5)

But, how did we get to that point? While it is a fairly long and detailed story covering not merely a few years of time, I will condense it as much as reasonable.

Jacob, who had been renamed Israel, had twelve sons. Joseph, the son of Jacob's favorite wife, Rachel, was also a favorite son of Jacob. Joseph was also a dreamer and the older brothers despised him. In Genesis 37:5-8, we learn:

⁵Joseph had a dream, and when he told it to his brothers, they hated him all the more. ⁶He said to them, "Listen to this dream I had: ⁷We were binding sheaves of grain out in the field when suddenly my sheaf rose and stood upright, while your sheaves gathered around mine and bowed down to it."

[8]His brothers said to him, "Do you intend to reign over us? Will you actually rule us?" And they hated him more because of his dream and what he had said.

Joseph had additional dreams wherein his brothers would bow down to him.

The brothers plotted to kill Joseph, but Ruben intervened to prevent that, and Judah suggested selling him. Joseph was sold to merchants traveling to Egypt. His price was twenty shekels of silver.

The beautiful robe Jacob had given to Joseph was torn and dipped in goat's blood. When the pieces were given to Jacob, he recognized it, and assumed that Joseph had been devoured by some wild animal. Jacob mourned the loss of Joseph for many days.

Meanwhile on arriving in Egypt, Joseph was sold to Pharaoh's captain of the guard named Potiphar. Potiphar's wife was attracted to Joseph, but when Joseph refused her attention, she lied to her husband and he had Joseph imprisoned.

While in prison Pharaoh's cupbearer and a baker were imprisoned along with Joseph. Each had a dream that troubled them and Joseph noticing their distress offered to help. He interpreted the cupbearer's dream that he would be released in three days and would go back to serve Pharaoh. He also interpreted the baker's dream to mean that he, too would be released in three days, but that Pharaoh would have him hanged and the birds would eat away his flesh. Joseph asked them to show favor to him after their release and help him to get released.

Both dreams came true and were fulfilled. However, the cupbearer did not remember Joseph and forgot about him at the time.

A full two years later Pharaoh had a dream, which none of his advisors could interpret. It was then that the cupbearer remembered Joseph and told Pharaoh about him. Pharaoh sent for Joseph. Joseph's interpretation is found Genesis 41:15-32. It reads as follows:

¹⁵Pharaoh said to Joseph, "I had a dream, and no one can interpret it. But I have heard it said of you that when you hear a dream you can interpret it."

¹⁶"I cannot do it," Joseph replied to Pharaoh, "but God will give Pharaoh the answer he desires."

¹⁷Then Pharaoh said to Joseph, "In my dream I was standing on the bank of the Nile, ¹⁸when out of the river there came up seven cows, fat and sleek, and they grazed among the reeds. ¹⁹After them, seven other cows came up—scrawny and very ugly and lean. I had never seen such ugly cows in all the land of Egypt. ²⁰The lean, ugly cows ate up the seven fat cows that came up first. ²¹But even after they ate them, no one could tell that they had done so; they looked just as ugly as before. Then I woke up.

²²"In my dream I saw seven heads of grain, full and good, growing on a single stalk. ²³After them, seven other heads sprouted—withered and thin and scorched by the east wind. ²⁴The thin heads of grain swallowed up the seven good heads. I told this to the magicians, but none of them could explain it to me."

²⁵Then Joseph said to Pharaoh, "The dreams of Pharaoh are one and the same. God has revealed to Pharaoh what he is about to do. ²⁶The seven good cows are seven years, and the seven good heads of grain are seven years; it is one and the same dream. ²⁷The seven lean, ugly cows that came up afterward are seven years, and so are the seven worthless heads of grain scorched by the east wind: They are seven years of famine.

²⁸"It is just as I said to Pharaoh: God has shown Pharaoh what he is about to do. ²⁹Seven years of great abundance are coming throughout the land of Egypt, ³⁰but seven years of famine will follow them. Then all the abundance in Egypt will be forgotten,

and the famine will ravage the land. ³¹The abundance in the land will not be remembered, because the famine that follows it will be so severe. ³²The reason the dream was given to Pharaoh in two forms is that the matter has been firmly decided by God, and God will do it soon.

Joseph suggested to Pharaoh that he appoint wise, discerning men and commissioners who would see to it that one-fifth of the grain harvest would be gathered each year and put in storage around the cities for use during the time of famine. This was not only a plan to avoid starvation, but also an economic plan to have grain that would bring big rewards to Egypt and to Pharaoh. The plan seemed good to Pharaoh and all the officials, but when no one was selected to serve in that capacity, Pharaoh determined that since God had made all this known to Joseph there was no one so discerning and wise as Joseph. The story continues in Genesis 41:41-43:

⁴¹So Pharaoh said to Joseph, "I hereby put you in charge of the whole land of Egypt." ⁴²Then Pharaoh took his signet ring from his finger and put it on Joseph's finger. He dressed him in robes of fine linen and put a gold chain around his neck. ⁴³He had him ride in a chariot as his second-in-command, and people shouted before him, "Make way!" Thus, he put him in charge of the whole land of Egypt.

Indeed, what the brothers and Potiphar's wife had done with evil intent has now turned into something incredibly good for Joseph.

The famine did come and those in Canaan were affected like others in the whole region. When Jacob learned that there was grain in Egypt, he sent his sons to buy some so that they could live and not die. Ten of the brothers made the journey, but Jacob kept his youngest child, the last son also by Rachel at home. This was Joseph's full bother Benjamin.

Joseph recognized his brothers, but they did not recognize him. He remembered the dreams he had about them bowing down to him. Joseph accused them of being spies and had them imprisoned for three days.

The entire story of the confrontation between Joseph's brothers and Joseph is interesting and intriguing and certainly is suggested reading. It is found in Genesis chapter 42 through chapter 50. In this we learn how the Israelites came to settle in Egypt and were permitted to stay, how they grew and prospered, and how Joseph in managing the affairs of Pharaoh was later able, through the sale of grain, to acquire all the land in Egypt for Pharaoh. The Egyptians sold their fields because of the famine and Pharaoh was able to purchase them with the grain that had been stored.

E. THE TROUBLE BEGINS

In Exodus 1:6-7, we find, "⁶Now Joseph and all his brothers and all that generation died, ⁷but the Israelites were exceedingly fruitful; they multiplied greatly, increased in numbers, and became so numerous that the land was filled with them."

Abraham had been told by God during the making of the Covenant that the Israelites would be enslaved in a foreign land. He was even told how long before they would be able to take the Promised Land. Many years had passed, and the new Pharaoh did not know or care much about Joseph. The Israelites had become too numerous to control. Slave masters were placed over them, and the people were oppressed and put into forced labor. However, the more they were oppressed the more they multiplied and spread so the Egyptians finally determined they would kill each newborn boy. If it was girl, they would let her live. Some of the midwives, however, feared God and did not do the King's bidding and let the boys live.

Moses was born during this time, and he was hidden for three months. When they could hide him no longer, he was placed in a basket which was then placed in some reeds along the bank of the Nile River. Much of this story is found in Exodus 2:5-10:

> [5]Then Pharaoh's daughter went down to the Nile to bathe, and her attendants were walking along the riverbank. She saw the basket among the reeds and sent her female slave to get it. [6]She opened it and saw the baby. He was crying, and she felt sorry for him. "This is one of the Hebrew babies," she said.
>
> [7]Then his sister asked Pharaoh's daughter, "Shall I go and get one of the Hebrew women to nurse the baby for you?" [8]"Yes, go," she answered. So, the girl went and got the baby's mother. [9]Pharaoh's daughter said to her, "Take this baby and nurse him for me, and I will pay you." The woman took the baby and nursed him. [10]When the child grew older, she took him to Pharaoh's daughter, and he became her son. She named him Moses, saying, "I drew him out of the water."

Moses was raised in the house of Pharaoh; he grew strong and was educated. He had learned of his own background as a Hebrew, and at about the age of forty he was observing his own people at labor. He saw an Egyptian beating a Hebrew and Moses killed the Egyptian.

Moses fled from Egypt and went to the land of Midian where he was helped by Jethro. Moses married Jethro's daughter, Zipporah.

Moses had been gone from Egypt for almost another forty years and conditions continued to get worse for the Israelites that were in Egypt. While tending the flock of Jethro, Moses had an encounter with God at a burning bush. In Exodus 3:5-10, we are told:

[5]"Do not come any closer," God said. "Take off your sandals, for the place where you are standing is holy ground." [6]Then he said, "I am the God of your father, the God of Abraham, the God of Isaac and the God of Jacob." At this, Moses hid his face, because he was afraid to look at God.

[7]The Lord said, "I have indeed seen the misery of my people in Egypt. I have heard them crying out because of their slave drivers, and I am concerned about their suffering. [8]So I have come down to rescue them from the hand of the Egyptians and to bring them up out of that land into a good and spacious land, a land flowing with milk and honey—the home of the Canaanites, Hittites, Amorites, Perizzites, Hivites and Jebusites. [9]And now the cry of the Israelites has reached me, and I have seen the way the Egyptians are oppressing them. [10]So now, go. I am sending you to Pharaoh to bring my people the Israelites out of Egypt."

Moses pled his inadequacies, but God would have none of it. God gave reassurances and promises, and God promised to perform several miracles and to strike the Egyptians. Another promise or prophecy that was fulfilled when they finally did leave Egypt is found in Exodus 3:21-22, which reads:

[21]"And I will make the Egyptians favorably disposed toward this people, so that when you leave you will not go empty-handed. [22]Every woman is to ask her neighbor and any woman living in her house for articles of silver and gold and for clothing, which you will put on your sons and daughters. And so you will plunder the Egyptians."

Moses does return to Egypt and joined with his brother Aaron who was a better speaker than Moses. The two worked together. Moses is now eighty years old and his brother is eighty-three. God tells Moses that in the eyes of Pharaoh he will be like a god and that Aaron would be his prophet. However, God also foretold that He would harden Pharaoh's heart, and Pharaoh would not let them leave. As a result, God promised to give more signs and wonders that would be very harmful to Egypt, but in the end God would bring the Israelites out of Egypt.

Moses and Aaron did go to Pharaoh and asked that he let the Israelites go into the desert for three days to have a festival and make sacrifices to God. See Exodus 5:1-3. Pharaoh refused and told them to have the people get back to work. He even made it harder for them.

Moses and Aaron returned to Pharaoh, and each time thereafter asked that he let the people go so they could make sacrifices to their Lord. Pharaoh refused and thus began the ten plagues. First, the waters of the Nile were turned to blood. Next came a plague of frogs, followed by gnats. Next came a plague of flies and then a plague on all the livestock of the Egyptians. These plagues did not adversely affect the Hebrews. The Lord then had Moses and Aaron take handfuls of soot from a furnace and toss it into the air in the presence of Pharaoh. It became fine dust which spread over Egypt and produced festering boils on men and animals. Pharaoh continued to refuse to let the Israelites leave, and next came a plague of hail. Then came a plague of locusts which devoured what little was still left including trees and crops growing in the fields. The next plague was one of darkness which lasted for three days, yet the Israelites had light in places where they lived.

Pharaoh then summoned Moses and allowed the people to go worship the Lord including the women and children, but the flocks and herds had to stay behind. Moses insisted that the livestock go with them, as they must have sacrifices and would have to use some of the animals in worshipping the Lord. However again Pharaoh's heart was hardened, and he would not let them leave. Finally, came the plague against the first born.

God told Moses that with this plague Pharaoh would let the people leave and will drive them out completely. He was told to tell the people that the men and women were to ask their neighbors for articles of silver and gold. The Lord had made the Egyptians favorably disposed toward the people and Moses. This would fulfill the promise that God had made to Moses while still in the land of Midian.

In Exodus 11:4-6, we read:

4So Moses said, "This is what the Lord says: 'About midnight I will go throughout Egypt. 5Every firstborn son in Egypt will die, from the firstborn son of Pharaoh, who sits on the throne, to the firstborn son of the female slave, who is at her hand mill, and all the firstborn of the cattle as well. 6There will be loud wailing throughout Egypt—worse than there has ever been or ever will be again. (Emphasis added)

Moses told these things to Pharaoh, but Pharaoh's heart was hardened, and he would not let the Israelites go out of his country.

F. THE PASSOVER-EXODUS

14"This is a day you are to *commemorate*; for the generations to come you shall celebrate it as *a festival* to the Lord—a lasting *ordinance.* 15For seven days you are to eat bread made without yeast. On the first day remove the yeast from your houses, for whoever eats anything with yeast in it from the first day through the seventh must be cut off from Israel. 16On the first day hold a sacred assembly, and another one on the seventh day. Do no work at all on these days, except to prepare food for everyone to eat; that is all you may do. Exodus 12:14-16 (Emphasis added)

The prescription for the Passover meal and for the Feast of Unleavened Bread was originally provided in Exodus 12. Beginning with verses 1-3, we read: "¹The Lord said to Moses and Aaron in Egypt, ²"This month is to be for you the first month, the first month of your year. ³Tell the whole community of Israel that on the tenth day of this month each man is to take a lamb for his family, one for each household." Continuing in verses 5-6, we find: "⁵The animals you choose must be year-old males without defect. ⁶Take care of them until the fourteenth day of the month, when all the members of the community of Israel must slaughter them at twilight."

For this special Passover night, the Israelites were also told in Exodus 12: 7-8 "⁷Then they are to take some of the blood and put it on the sides and tops of the doorframes of the houses where they eat the lambs. ⁸That same night they are to eat the meat roasted over the fire, along with bitter herbs, and bread made without yeast."

Before moving on, let us note that this meal is the memorial meal for the Abrahamic covenant. We must also note that part of the sacrificial blood was to be put over the doorframes to identify those covered by the covenant. Later in keeping the Passover, the blood of the perfect lambs was used to atone for, or "cover" the sins of the people for a time; however, it was not until the perfect Lamb of God, Jesus Christ, was sacrificed that the blood of the New Covenant permanently "washed away" man's sin for those who believed, accepted, and followed Jesus. A cutting and the shedding of blood were part of the custom of covenant making.

To avoid some confusion later, I want to reiterate that the Jews begin their day at sundown. They were to slaughter their lamb at twilight which would have been around three o'clock in the afternoon. They would have roasted it by fire and had their meal after sundown. Therefore, if they slaughtered the lamb on the fourteenth day of the first month, they ate it just after sundown at the beginning of the fifteenth day.

For this first Passover meal, they were to do it in haste, and be ready to leave the next day. Exodus 12, verse 11, provides: "¹¹This is how you are to eat it: with your cloak tucked into your belt, your sandals on your feet and your staff in your hand. Eat it in haste; it is the Lord's Passover." One other restriction on the celebration of this Passover meal is written in Exodus 12:46 where we find: "'⁴⁶It must be eaten inside the house; take none of the meat outside the house. *Do not break any of the bones.*'" Exodus 12:46 (Emphasis added)

The Israelites were told to obey the instructions as a lasting ordinance for themselves and their descendants, and when they enter the land the Lord has promised to give them, they must observe this ceremony. They were told that when their children would ask what this ceremony means, they were to tell them it is the Passover sacrifice to the Lord who passed over the houses of the Israelites in Egypt and spared our homes when God struck down the Egyptians.

The Egyptians were anxious for the Israelites to leave, otherwise they were in fear that all might die. As had been foretold, they did give their silver and gold and clothing to the Israelites as they left. Thus, the Exodus begins.

The Israelites journeyed from Rameses to Sukkoth. There were about six hundred thousand men on foot besides women and children. Many other people went with them, and they also had large droves of livestock. Some estimates have indicated that including men, women, and children, there would have been roughly two million people in this Exodus. The potential logistics needed for such an adventure makes me shutter. It is certainly beyond anything man could do. The Exodus has to be one of the greatest miracles of all times.

Abraham had been told during the making of the Covenant with him how long the Israelites would be in Egypt. Exodus 12:41 tells us: "⁴¹At the end of the 430 years, to the very day, all the Lord's divisions left Egypt." It is unimaginable that in a group of two million people of all ages and conditions, traveling with little food and water, and under the conditions of hot and cold, that none were reported to be sick or unable to move. *The perfect lamb each ate must have provided real power and healing.* (My comment).

However, it did not take long before many were beginning to complain about the conditions. Immediately, God provided a cloud by day for shade and a pillar of fire by night for light and some heat. See, Exodus 13: 22-22. This was something definitely above Moses's pay grade.

The complaining continued, and in Exodus 14:11-14, we read:

[11]They said to Moses, "Was it because there were no graves in Egypt that you brought us to the desert to die? What have you done to us by bringing us out of Egypt? [12]Didn't we say to you in Egypt, 'Leave us alone; let us serve the Egyptians'? It would have been better for us to serve the Egyptians than to die in the desert!"

[13]Moses answered the people, "Do not be afraid. Stand firm and you will see the deliverance the Lord will bring you today. The Egyptians you see today you will never see again. [14]The Lord will fight for you; you need only to be still."

We are told that Pharaoh's heart was hardened again, and after learning that the Israelites had left, he could not stand the thought of losing their services. He sent his army after them to bring them back. God had the Israelites move to a location where Pharaoh's army could be trapped. I have no idea exactly where the crossing took place or how deep the water might have been. There is an area north of the Gulf of Suez, which is the West branch of the Red Sea, which has several smaller bodies of water where they might have crossed. They might have moved north to an area known as the "Sea of Reeds."

Some maps of the Exodus route and the wanderings show several possible places where the crossing most likely occurred.

Whatever, Moses raised his rod again and held it while an East wind divided the waters, and the Israelites were allowed to cross on dry land. When Pharaoh's army followed, the waters came together, and his army was destroyed. The story of the crossing can be found in Exodus 14:15-31.

Following the crossing there was much rejoicing, but in time the fussing began again due to a lack of water and food. As they moved down the Sinai Peninsula to the area of Marah and Elam, God through Moses provided water, manna, and quail. The water came forth when Moses was instructed to strike a rock at Horeb with his staff. He then named the place Massah and Meribah. This story can be found Exodus 17:5-7.

I believe this would be a good time to quote Psalm 81. While I would urge you to read the entire Psalm, I will only quote verses 7-10.

7In your distress you called and I rescued you,
I answered you out of a thundercloud;
I tested you at the *waters of Meribah.*
8Hear me, my people, and I will warn you—
if you would only listen to me, Israel!
9You shall have no foreign god among you;
you shall not worship any god other than me.
10*I am the Lord your God,*
who brought you up out of Egypt.
Open wide your mouth and I will fill it. (Emphasis added)

The Psalmist is explaining how God had heard the distress of the people and He answered them and provided the water at Meribah. God again tells them what He will do if they listen to Him, have no other God but Him, and recognize that God is the Lord who brought them out of Egypt.

The quoted text concludes, "Open wide your mouth and I will fill it." In the Preface for this book, I mentioned that I had listened to some tapes produced by Malcom Smith. One of the word pictures he presented in one of the tapes came from this verse. Smith compared the situation to what being in a covenant relationship with God could be. He used the example of baby birds. You can see them in a nest and all you see is their open mouths. They are absolutely helpless, but the parents bring food and put it in their mouths. That is how being a covenant partner with God can bless us. When we are at our weakest, God can do the most for us. Believe, obey God's laws, and be blessed.

If you read the remainder of Psalm 81 you will also find that the people do not follow God's commands, they are stiff necked and disobedient, and as a result he punishes them. That, too, is part of being in a covenant relationship. There are blessings when you follow the terms of the covenant, and there are curses put upon you when you violate those terms.

While traveling through the desert the Israelites were totally helpless and at the mercy of God. However, He could and did take care of them by providing food, water, what clothing they needed, and what shelter they had to have. This situation lasted for forty years.

The Israelites arrived at the desert of Sinai where they camped near the front of the mountain. In Exodus 19:3-5, we are told:

³Then Moses went up to God, and the Lord called to him from the mountain and said, "This is what you are to say to the descendants of Jacob and what you are to tell the people of Israel: ⁴"You yourselves have seen what I did to Egypt, and how I carried you on eagles' wings and brought you to myself. ⁵Now if you obey me fully and keep my covenant, then out of all nations you will be my treasured possession.

I find the following passages very significant. In Exodus 19:16-20, we read:

¹⁶On the morning of the third day there was thunder and lightning, with a thick cloud over the mountain, and a very loud trumpet blast. Everyone in the camp trembled. ¹⁷Then Moses led the people out of the camp to meet with God, and they stood at the foot of the mountain. ¹⁸Mount Sinai was covered with smoke, because the Lord descended on it in fire. The smoke billowed up from it like smoke from a furnace, and the whole mountain trembled violently. ¹⁹As the sound of the trumpet grew louder and louder, Moses spoke, and the voice of God answered him.

²⁰The Lord descended to the top of Mount Sinai and called Moses to the top of the mountain. So Moses went up.

From these passages, I can easily calculate that when this occurred there had been roughly forty-nine days from the time the Israelites left Egypt. They begin leaving the fifteenth day of the first month of their religious calendar, known as Nissan. That month has thirty days. Counting the fifteenth day as the first day there would have been sixteen days used in that month. The next month has twenty-nine days and that would produce at least forty-five. They entered the desert of Sinai on the first day of the third month which would then be forty-six days, and we learn in verse sixteen that it was on the third day after being there when Moses went up to the mountain. Somehow, I believe that in God's timing, there had been fifty days between the time the Israelites began leaving Egypt, or perhaps from the time they crossed the water until what occurred at Mount Sinai. We are told that at that time there was thunder and lightning and a thick cloud on the mountain, fire, shaking of the ground, and a loud sound of trumpets. We will learn later in Acts Chapter 2, in the chapter in this book on The Holy Spirit, that on the day of Pentecost following the death and resurrection of Jesus, many of these same displays took place in Jerusalem. Remember these points for later.

It was on this visit to the mountain that Moses received the Ten Commandments. See Exodus, Chapter 20. Later, Moses was given many other laws including the requirement for three annual convocations, the requirements for a mobile tabernacle, the vestments for priests, and how to treat fellow Israelites and strangers. The description of these laws, among others, can be found in Exodus Chapters 24-40.

Many of you will be familiar with the fact that following Moses's first forty-day visit to the mountain, the Israelites had built a golden calf and were worshipping it. In Moses's anger and disappointment, he broke the Ten Commandments. He later had to return to the mountain for another forty days where he received them again.

God was also angry with the Israelites and their worship of the golden calf idol. He threatened to destroy the Israelites at that time. However, Moses pleads their case, and in Exodus 32:11-13, we see:

> 11But Moses sought the favor of the Lord his God. "Lord," he said, "why should your anger burn against your people, whom you brought out of Egypt with great power and a mighty hand? 12Why should the Egyptians say, 'It was with evil intent that he brought them out, to kill them in the mountains and to wipe them off the face of the earth'? Turn from your fierce anger; relent and do not bring disaster on your people. 13Remember your servants Abraham, Isaac, and Israel, to whom you swore by your own self: 'I will make your descendants as numerous as the stars in the sky and I will give your descendants all this land I promised them, and it will be their inheritance forever.'

God remembered the covenant and relented in verse 14.

In all this God made His covenant with Moses, but He did not forget the covenant with Abraham.

In Exodus 33:1-2 we are told:

¹Then the Lord said to Moses, "Leave this place, you and the people you brought up out of Egypt and go up to the land I promised on oath to Abraham, Isaac and Jacob, saying, 'I will give it to your descendants.' ²I will send an angel before you and drive out the Canaanites, Amorites, Hittites, Perizzites, Hivites and Jebusites.

Despite this promise, when the Israelites got close to the Promised Land, they became fearful of the tribes and groups they would meet there. They did not go in, although God had promised to drive out those that were there. As a result of this disobedience, the Israelites wondered for many more years for a total of forty. When the wandering ended and they finally got to their Promised Land, Moses was now 120 years old. He was not allowed to enter, but from the mountain across the Jordan River he was able to see some of the Promised Land. Moses died and was buried there.

G. THE LAW REQUIRING SEVEN FEASTS

God had delivered the Israelites from Egypt and had taken care of them through forty years of wondering. He provided cover, food, water, clothing, and all that they needed. During the time of the wondering, they had no lands, they had no crops of their own, they just kept moving. Now they are ready to enter the Promised Land, and God orders the Israelites to assemble in an appointed place and at an appointed time three times each year for a holy convocation to remember all that He had done for them. We find this in later chapters of Exodus, but more specifically in Leviticus 23 and Deuteronomy 16. Once the Israelites are settled in the land, the Holy convocations are to take place in Jerusalem. The law pertaining to the first convocation and the first three required feasts is found in Leviticus 23:4-11. It provides and requires:

[4]"these are the Lord's appointed festivals, the sacred assemblies you are to proclaim at their appointed times: [5]The Lord's Passover begins at twilight on the fourteenth day of the first month. [6]On the fifteenth day of that month the Lord's Festival of Unleavened Bread begins; for seven days you must eat bread made without yeast. [7]On the first day hold a sacred assembly and do no regular work. [8]For seven days present a food offering to the Lord. And on the seventh day hold a sacred assembly and do no regular work."

OFFERING THE FIRST FRUITS

[9]The Lord said to Moses, [10]"Speak to the Israelites and say to them: *'When you enter the land I am going to give you and you reap its harvest, bring to the priest a sheaf of the first grain you harvest.* [11]*He is to wave the sheaf before the Lord* so it will be accepted on your behalf; the priest is to wave it *on the day after the Sabbath."* (Emphasis added)

Even when the Passover meal was first prescribed in Exodus 12, God told Moses that this was to be a holy convocation to remember what He had done for the Israelites. They were actually to take a perfect unblemished male lamb on the tenth day of the first month, inspect it for three days, and then slaughter it at twilight on the fourteenth. They would then roast it and eat it on the fifteenth. That was also the beginning of the requirement that they use nothing but unleavened bread for seven days.

Now that they can have crops of their own, they have added the Feast of First Fruits, so during this first required convocation they actually celebrate three feasts: Passover, Unleavened Bread, and First Fruits. You might note that First Fruits is always celebrated during the seven-day period of unleavened bread on the day after the Jewish Sabbath, whenever that might fall within the week. Since the Jewish Sabbath starts at sundown on what we refer to as Friday and ends at sunset on what we would call Saturday, *the Feast of First Fruits will always be on what we refer to as Sunday or at least from sundown on Saturday through sunset on Sunday. It will be on that day annually no matter what time or what day Passover occurs and Unleavened Bread begins.* (My emphasis)

When the Israelites obeyed all their laws, including the requirements for these three convocations, they were blessed, and when they neglected them they had problems such as the loss of the ten Northern tribes of Israel, the destruction of Jerusalem, and the Babylon captivity. God has also told them, He would disperse them throughout the earth through deportation, and conquering armies. See Deuteronomy 28:64-67 and Ezekiel 22:15. However, God also promised to finally return them from around the world. See Deuteronomy 30:3 and Isaiah 11:11. (Remember these prophesies for later consideration when reading chapter 8 on "The Future.")

Bad kings ignored the feasts, but the good kings restored them. It was the observance of all the commandments that preserved the covenant relationship. Keeping the feasts was and still is important.

One thing I remember from the Rick Godwin tapes was his reference to Psalm 89:15 found in the Amplified Bible. It reads:

> [15]Blessed (happy, fortunate, to be envied) are the people who know the joyful sound [who understand and appreciate the spiritual blessings symbolized by the feasts]; they walk, O Lord, in the light *and* favor of Your countenance!

This passage illustrates just how significant observing the feasts can and should be.

The second convocation also to be held in Jerusalem annually was known as the Feast of Weeks or Harvest, and as we know it today, Pentecost. It occurred fifty days after the Feast of First Fruits. Leviticus 23:15-16, provides:

[15]From the day after the Sabbath, the day you brought the sheaf of the wave offering, count off seven full weeks. [16]Count off fifty days up to the day after the seventh Sabbath, and then present an offering of new grain to the Lord.

We might note that neither First Fruits nor Pentecost were prescribed until after the Israelites entered the Promised Land. The only thing they were required to do when leaving Egypt was to eat the sacrificial lamb and eat no leavened bread for seven days. First Fruits just might be analogous to the crossing of the Sea with the ultimate death, burial, and resurrection of Jesus Christ. The Israelites entered the water but came out alive. The Egyptians who followed died on the spot with a burial, but no resurrection. Admittedly, I have no real idea of just why God would prescribe the Feast of First Fruits the way He did, but this is something to think about.

Likewise, Pentecost was not established until the Israelites could enter the Promised Land. My timing of the trek from Egypt to Mt. Sinai was from Passover to the mountain, and Pentecost is now to be counted from First Fruits, or perhaps the crossing of the Sea. God may well have used these events for establishing the two memorial feasts.

The final convocation occurs in the fall at the final harvest time. It, too, is a three-fold feast beginning with the Feast of Trumpets followed by the Day of Atonement, and finally the Seven Day Feast of Tabernacles. From Leviticus 23:23-25 we learn:

[23]The Lord said to Moses, [24]"Say to the Israelites: 'On the first day of the seventh month you are to have a day of Sabbath rest, a sacred assembly commemorated with trumpet blasts. [25]Do no regular work, but present a food offering to the Lord.'"

The seventh month is part of the Jewish religious calendar. It is also the first month of its civil calendar, and the Feast of Trumpets falls on the first day of the Jewish civil New Year, which is also known as Rosh Hashanah, or Tishrei 1.

The requirements continue in Leviticus 23:26-32 and it shows us:

²⁶The Lord said to Moses, ²⁷"The tenth day of this seventh month is the Day of Atonement. Hold a sacred assembly and deny yourselves and present a food offering to the Lord. ²⁸Do not do any work on that day, because it is the Day of Atonement, when atonement is made for you before the Lord your God. ²⁹Those who do not deny themselves on that day must be cut off from their people. ³⁰I will destroy from among their people anyone who does any work on that day. ³¹You shall do no work at all. This is to be a lasting ordinance for the generations to come, wherever you live. ³²It is a day of Sabbath rest for you, and you must deny yourselves. From the evening of the ninth day of the month until the following evening you are to observe your Sabbath."

The Day of Atonement is the holiest day of the year in the Jewish community. It comes on Tishrei 10 and is also known as Yom Kippur. No matter what day of the week it falls on, it is considered a Sabbath in the sense that the Jewish people must rest and do no work.

The third feast of the three held during this final annual convocation is the Feast of Tabernacles, or sometimes known as the Feast of Booths commemorating when the Jews lived in Booths as they were wandering about. Leviticus 23:33-43 provides:

³³The Lord said to Moses, ³⁴"Say to the Israelites: 'On the fifteenth day of the seventh month the Lord's Festival of Tabernacles begins, and it lasts for seven days. ³⁵The first day is a sacred assembly; do no regular work. ³⁶For seven days present food offerings to the Lord, and on the eighth day hold a sacred assembly and present

a food offering to the Lord. It is the closing special assembly; do no regular work . . . ³⁹ "'So beginning with the fifteenth day of the seventh month, after you have gathered the crops of the land, celebrate the festival to the Lord for seven days; the first day is a day of Sabbath rest, and the eighth day also is a day of Sabbath rest. ⁴⁰On the first day you are to take branches from luxuriant trees—from palms, willows and other leafy trees—and rejoice before the Lord your God for seven days. ⁴¹Celebrate this as a festival to the Lord for seven days each year. This is to be a lasting ordinance for the generations to come; celebrate it in the seventh month. ⁴²Live in temporary shelters for seven days: All native-born Israelites are to live in such shelters ⁴³so your descendants will know that I had the Israelites live in temporary shelters when I brought them out of Egypt. I am the Lord your God.'"

See also Exodus 23:14-17.

Two other significant laws are provided in Leviticus 25, and these were to be observed just as faithfully as the three convocations with the Seven Feasts. These are the Sabbatical Year and the Year of Jubilee. In Leviticus 25:1-4, God required:

¹The Lord said to Moses at Mount Sinai, ²"Speak to the Israelites and say to them: 'When you enter the land I am going to give you, the land itself must observe a Sabbath to the Lord. ³For six years sow your fields, and for six years prune your vineyards and gather their crops. ⁴But in the seventh year the land is to have a year of Sabbath rest, a Sabbath to the Lord. Do not sow your fields or prune your vineyards.'

See also Exodus 23:10-11.

The Year of Jubilee is found in Leviticus 25:8-12:

[8]Count off seven Sabbath years—seven times seven years—so that the seven Sabbath years amount to a period of forty-nine years. [9]Then have the trumpet sounded everywhere on the tenth day of the seventh month; on the Day of Atonement sound the trumpet throughout your land. [10]Consecrate the fiftieth year and proclaim liberty throughout the land to all its inhabitants. It shall be a jubilee for you; each of you is to return to your family property and to your own clan. [11]The fiftieth year shall be a jubilee for you; do not sow and do not reap what grows of itself or harvest the untended vines. [12]For it is a jubilee and is to be holy for you; eat only what is taken directly from the fields.

The seven-year sabbatical also applies to the cancelling of debts. We find in Deuteronomy 15:1-2:

At the end of every seven years you must cancel debts. [2]This is how it is to be done: Every creditor shall cancel any loan they have made to a fellow Israelite. They shall not require payment from anyone among their own people, because the Lord's time for canceling debts has been proclaimed.

H. OLD TESTAMENT PROPHESIES

While I intend to concentrate primarily upon the prophesies foretelling the coming of Jesus, his life, and certainly some for the end times, before getting into those, I want to mention one other prophesy pertaining to God's declaration of blessings and curses. This prophesy ties right into the Sabbath rest for land.

In Leviticus 26:33-35, we read:

³³I will scatter you among the nations and will draw out my sword and pursue you. Your land will be laid waste, and your cities will lie in ruins. ³⁴Then the land will enjoy its Sabbath years all the time that it lies desolate and you are in the country of your enemies; then the land will rest and enjoy its Sabbaths. ³⁵All the time that it lies desolate, the land will have the rest it did not have during the Sabbaths you lived in it.

This message was given to Moses, perhaps around 1400 BC. After several years, the Israelites began disobeying and ignoring the laws of God, including that they must give the land a rest every seventh year. Certainly, the days before modern agriculture this was good agricultural science. Nevertheless, the Israelites ignored this requirement for many years. During that time, they were warned to repent and to follow God's laws. The Northern Kingdom of Israel was attacked by the Assyrians, totally destroyed, and the people taken as captives or scattered. The Judeans ignored the warning and continued in their disobedient and evil ways.

Finally, Judah was attacked by the Babylonians. Daniel and a few others were captured around 605 BC, and Ezekiel and about ten thousand were taken around 597 BC. Finally, Jerusalem and the temple were destroyed in 586 BC. (You will notice that in this counting of years, we appear to be counting backward, since with the common calendar, we are counting down to the time of Jesus—Anno Domini.)

The survivors were taken into captivity and relocated to Babylon. That period of captivity lasted for 70 years. It is easy to do the math by dividing 70 into 490. The answer is that the land was allowed to rest for the 70 Sabbaths which had been ignored. The disobedience apparently began during the time when the new country was ruled by judges and just before the first king, Saul. Some kings were good and obedient, such as David, but most allowed evil and disobedience to enter. In some way, God calculated the time, and gave the land a rest for seventy years.

This situation and other similar situations provide more evidence that there is a God, who is in control. Also, He has a covenant relationship with His people. When they obey they are blessed and when they deny and disobey His commands and laws they are punished. The situation was foretold long before it happened. It is no mere coincidence.

Many prophesies pertaining to the coming of Jesus are found in the Old Testament and they have been fulfilled. Earlier we learned in Genesis that He would come through the line of Abraham, Isaac, and Jacob, and that He would be a descendent of Judah. We were also told in the prescription for the Passover that no bone was to be broken. See also Psalm 34:20. Psalm 22:14-16 announced that He would be crucified, and further in that Psalm we learn that those gloating over Him will divide His clothing and cast lots for it. See verses 17-18.

Several prophesies can be found in the writings of the Prophet Isaiah. He announced that He would be born of a virgin. (Isaiah 7:14) One of the most familiar is found Isaiah 9:6. It reads: "For to us a child is born, to us a son is given, and the government will be on his shoulders. And he will be called Wonderful Counselor, Mighty God, Everlasting Father, Prince of Peace."

In Isaiah Chapter 11, we learn that Christ will come from the roots and the branch of Jesse. Jesse was King David's father. In God's covenant with David, He promised that the Abrahamic covenant would attach to David's lineage.

We are told in Isaiah 11:2 that: "The Spirit of the Lord will rest on him—the *Spirit of wisdom and of understanding*, the Spirit of counsel and of might, the Spirit of the knowledge and fear of the Lord." (Emphasis added) Obviously, Jesus was to have it all, not merely a Word of Knowledge or a Word of Wisdom.

In Isaiah 52 we are told of Christ suffering in verses 13 and 14 which read:

¹³See, my servant will act wisely;

he will be raised and lifted up and highly exalted.

¹⁴Just as there were many who were appalled at him—

his appearance was so disfigured beyond that of any human being

and his form marred beyond human likeness—

The description continues in Isaiah 53 we find in verses 3-7 more prophesies about Jesus. These verses provide:

³He was despised and rejected by mankind,

a man of suffering, and familiar with pain.

Like one from whom people hide their faces

he was despised, and we held him in low esteem.

⁴Surely he took up our pain

and bore our suffering,

yet we considered him punished by God,

stricken by him, and afflicted.

⁵But he was pierced for our transgressions,

he was crushed for our iniquities;

the punishment that brought us peace was on him,

and by his wounds we are healed.

⁶We all, like sheep, have gone astray,

each of us has turned to our own way;

and the Lord has laid on him

the iniquity of us all.

⁷He was oppressed and afflicted,

yet he did not open his mouth;

he was led like a lamb to the slaughter,

and as a sheep before its shearers is silent,
so he did not open his mouth.

These descriptions are parallel with the life of Jesus, His mission, His horrible suffering and death to atone for the sins of all mankind. This is more history before it happened.

These prophesies were all made hundreds of years before the birth of Christ. Isaiah and Micah both lived and prophesied around 700 BC . . .

The fact that Jesus would be born in Bethlehem was also prophesied. In Micah 5:2 we read: "²'But you, Bethlehem Ephrathah, though you are small among the clans of Judah, out of you will come for me one who will be ruler over Israel, whose origins are from of old, from ancient times.'"

Isaiah also prophesied that John the Baptist would lead the way, and in Isaiah 40:3-5 we find:

³A voice of one calling: "In the wilderness prepare the way for the Lord; make straight in the desert a highway for our God."
⁵And the glory of the Lord will be revealed, and all people will see it together. For the mouth of the Lord has spoken."

Further Isaiah prophesied in Chapter 56:3, "³Let no foreigner who is bound to the Lord say, 'The Lord will surely exclude me from his people.'" Here he is prophesying that through Jesus, salvation will come for others and not just the Israelites.

The prophet Jeremiah declares that there will be a New Covenant and that we will no longer need the law (the Ten Commandments), as with the coming of the Holy Spirit, the law will be written on their hearts. In Jeremiah 31:31-34 we read:

[31]"The days are coming," declares the Lord, "when I will make a new covenant with the people of Israel and with the people of Judah. [32]It will not be like the covenant I made with their ancestors when I took them by the hand to lead them out of Egypt, because they broke my covenant, though I was a husband to them," declares the Lord. [33]"This is the covenant I will make with the people of Israel after that time," declares the Lord. "I will put my law in their minds and write it on their hearts. I will be their God, and they will be my people. [34]No longer will they teach their neighbor, or say to one another, 'Know the Lord,' because they will all know me, from the least of them to the greatest," declares the Lord. "For I will forgive their wickedness."

With what has been written, I will conclude my summary of the Old Testament or Covenant. Much more could be said, but I hope to have laid a foundation for understanding what law and prophesies Jesus had to fulfill, and, indeed, did fulfill.

I do hope you now understand what a covenant is all about, and how they are (were) made with sacrifice and even blood. We rarely hear anything about such in our churches today, and some churches seem to avoid the mention of "blood."

It is my hope, too, that you will understand and appreciate the reality and power of God, our creator. With all of the miracles and fulfilled prophesies, we must know that what is written in the Holy Bible are not just made-up stories. None of what we have learned were mere coincidences. With so many different writers, writing over so many years, and in three languages, it all fits too well to have been made up, except by some divine, overseeing power.

In the Old Testament, we learn about the love of God for His people. There is much wisdom to be learned in the Psalms and Proverbs, as well as in books such as Job. *One profound theme clarifies, defines, and explains wisdom and understanding, and where and how we find them? In simple terms, wisdom is found in the fear of the Lord, and to turn from evil is understanding.* Understanding follows wisdom like day follows the night.

†

CHAPTER 5

THE NEW TESTAMENT-COVENANT

"¹⁶For God so loved the world that he gave his one and only Son, that whoever believes in him shall not perish but have eternal life. ¹⁷For God did not send his Son into the world to condemn the world, but to save the world through him."

JOHN 3:16-17

While there are many verses in the New Testament which could have been used to introduce the subject, there are probably none more appropriate than John 3:16-17. For years under the Old Testament law, people had been sacrificing those unblemished four-legged lambs, millions of them, but they could not atone as a blood sacrifice for the sins of everyone forever, and especially for the Gentiles and those not covered by the old covenant. John 3:16-17 tells that God himself came in the form of Jesus, as God in the flesh, to become the blood sacrifice for the new covenant and He is doing this not to condemn the world but to save it. That is what the New Testament is all about. Perhaps it should be noted, too, that this was done according to God's perfect timing.

There was essentially peace on earth, although it was an enforced peace by the Romans. There was generally a common language, and Israel was somewhat in the center of worldly affairs.

A. THE BIRTH OF JESUS AND THE EARLY YEARS

What we know about Jesus, His birth, and his early years can be found generally in the first and second chapters of the Gospels of Matthew and Luke. Matthew 1:1-17 recites the 42 generations from Abraham to Jesus, an amazing genealogy. As for his birth, we read in Matthew 1:18-23:

> [18]This is how the birth of Jesus the Messiah came about: His mother Mary was pledged to be married to Joseph, but before they came together, she was found to be pregnant through the Holy Spirit. [19]Because Joseph her husband was faithful to the law, and yet did not want to expose her to public disgrace, he had in mind to divorce her quietly.
>
> [20]But after he had considered this, an angel of the Lord appeared to him in a dream and said, "Joseph son of David, do not be afraid to take Mary home as your wife, because what is conceived in her is from the Holy Spirit. [21]She will give birth to a son, and you are to give him the name Jesus, because he will save his people from their sins."
>
> [22]All this took place to fulfill what the Lord had said through the prophet: [23]"The virgin will conceive and give birth to a son, and they will call him Immanuel" *(which means "God with us")*.

Joseph must have been a very special person. Joseph and Mary were engaged and here she is pregnant with a child. Under the conditions in those days, he could have had her stoned to death, and we would have had no Mary or Jesus. However, an angel did speak to him to tell him what was happening, and he obeyed. One of the prophesies was, therefore, fulfilled. Jesus would be born of a virgin.

Mary and Joseph were from the line of Judah. Rome required that people return to their ancestral homes to be enrolled in a census and for tax purposes. Just prior to the birth of Jesus, they traveled from Nazareth to Bethlehem. That, also fulfilled a prophesy that the Messiah would be born in Bethlehem.

Wise men (perhaps astrologers) from eastern countries came to Jerusalem and Bethlehem to seek the newborn "King of Jews." They asked King Herod where they could find the baby, and Herod told them to return and let him know where Jesus could be located. This was not Herod's intent, however, as he was determined to destroy any baby that might become a king to replace him. He, therefore, ordered that all infants under the age of two be killed. Joseph was told in a dream what was going to happen and was told to flee the area. He took Mary and the baby and went to Egypt where they stayed until Herod died. When they returned, they located in their former home of Nazareth. This would fulfill another prophesy which indicated that Jesus would also be known as the Nazarene.

We next learn that when Jesus was twelve years old he traveled with his parents in a group from Nazareth to Jerusalem for Passover. Jesus remained at the temple with the priest and teachers. One might say that Jesus was having a very special "bar mitzvah." We find in Luke 2:46-47: "⁴⁶After three days they found him in the temple courts, sitting among the teachers, listening to them and asking them questions. ⁴⁷Everyone who heard him was amazed at his understanding and his answers." It is clear that Jesus had an exceptional knowledge of the Old Testament law and the prophesies.

B. JESUS PREPARES FOR HIS MINISTRY

John the Baptist began preparing the way for Jesus. This, too, fulfilled another prophesy. In Luke 3:4-6, we find:

⁴As it is written in the book of the words of Isaiah the prophet: "A voice of one calling in the wilderness, 'Prepare the way for

the Lord, make straight paths for him. ⁵Every valley shall be filled in, every mountain and hill made low. The crooked roads shall become straight, the rough ways smooth. ⁶And all people will see God's salvation.'"

Many of the people wondered if John was, in fact, the Christ. However, in Luke 3:16 John set the record straight. The passage reads, "¹⁶John answered them all, 'I baptize you with water. But one who is more powerful than I will come, the straps of whose sandals I am not worthy to untie. He will baptize you with the Holy Spirit and fire."

We find the same passage in John 1:26, and then we read in John 1:29: "²⁹the next day John saw Jesus coming toward him and said, 'Look, the *Lamb of God*, who takes away the sin of the world!" (Emphasis added)

Jesus came to John for baptism, and following the baptism we learn, in John 1: 32-34:

> ³²Then John gave this testimony: "I saw the Spirit come down from heaven as a dove and remain on him. ³³And I myself did not know him, but the one who sent me to baptize with water told me, 'The man on whom you see the Spirit come down and remain is the one who will baptize with the Holy Spirit.' ³⁴I have seen and I testify that this is God's Chosen One."

We find this same testimony in Matthew 3:16-17.

After Jesus had been baptized, he departed and went to the desert where he fasted for forty days and nights. Following that period, he was hungry and was tempted by Satan. We learn in Matthew 4:3-11:

> ³The tempter came to him and said, "If you are the Son of God, tell these stones to become bread." ⁴*Jesus answered, "It is written:*

'Man shall not live on bread alone, but on every word that comes from the mouth of God.'"

⁵Then the devil took him to the holy city and had him stand on the highest point of the temple. ⁶"If you are the Son of God," he said, "throw yourself down. For it is written: "'He will command his angels concerning you, and they will lift you up in their hands, so that you will not strike your foot against a stone.'" ⁷*Jesus answered him, "It is also written: 'Do not put the Lord your God to the test.'"* ⁸Again, the devil took him to a very high mountain and showed him all the kingdoms of the world and their splendor. ⁹"All this I will give you," he said, "if you will bow down and worship me."

¹⁰Jesus said to him, *"Away from me, Satan! For it is written: 'Worship the Lord your God and serve him only.*"

¹¹Then the devil left him, and angels came and attended him. (Emphasis added)

As you can see, the Devil gave three temptations and in response to each Jesus referred to the writings of the Old Testament and then Satan departed and left him alone. Obviously, Jesus knew the law and the prophesies of the Old Testament. It also seems clear that each knew who and what the other party was.

As Jesus began preparing for His ministry, He began selecting his disciples. He first found Simon, whom Jesus named Peter, and his brother Andrew, both fishermen. He urged them to follow him whereby he would make them fishers of men. Next, He recruited James and John, sons of Zebedee, also fishermen. Later he got Philip, Bartholomew, Thomas, and Matthew, the tax collector. He got another James, known as the son of Alpheus, and Thaddaeus. Finally, he got Simon the zealot, and Judas Iscariot, who later betrayed Him. These made the twelve.

C. THE THREE-YEAR MINISTRY OF JESUS

The numerous miracles, wonders, healings, and teachings of Jesus during his three-year ministry can be found in the Gospels: Matthew, Mark, Luke, and John. For the purposes of this writing, I will only be able to summarize and highlight a few events and encourage you to read the four Gospels for yourself. These are not directly related to my primary purpose of showing how Jesus fulfilled the laws and created the "new covenant" with His own blood.

Jesus taught in synagogues, in the fields, and on mountains. He preached to large crowds and small crowds alike. He was on a mountain when he gave the sermon describing the "Beatitudes" (Be Attitudes). They are found in Matthew 5:1-12. Jesus used common items such as salt and light that people clearly understood in making analogies. He taught that we should love our enemies, and that we must help the needy. He told us how to pray when giving us "The Lord's Prayer" which can be found in Matthew 6:9-13. It reads:

> 9"This, then, is how you should pray: 'Our Father in heaven, hallowed be your name, 10your kingdom come, your will be done, on earth as it is in heaven. 11Give us today our daily bread. 12And forgive us our debts, as we also have forgiven our debtors. 13And lead us not into temptation, but deliver us from the evil one.'

Following the recitation of the Lord's Prayer He also explained that if we are to be forgiven by God, we must be forgiving of our fellow man. As to judging others, Jesus taught in Matthew 7: 3-5:

> 3Why do you look at the speck of sawdust in your brother's eye and pay no attention to the plank in your own eye? 4How can you say to your brother, 'Let me take the speck out of your eye,' when all the time there is a plank in your own eye? 5You

hypocrite, first take the plank out of your own eye, and then you will see clearly to remove the speck from your brother's eye.

Jesus urged us to store up our treasures in heaven and made it clear that where our treasure is there will our heart be also. He pointed out that we need not worry about having enough clothes or food. In making an analogy with birds and flowers He is quoted in Matthew 6:26-30:

[26]Look at the birds of the air; they do not sow or reap or store away in barns, and yet your heavenly Father feeds them. Are you not much more valuable than they? [27]Can any one of you by worrying add a single hour to your life?

[28]"And why do you worry about clothes? See how the flowers of the field grow. They do not labor or spin. [29]Yet I tell you that not even Solomon in all his splendor was dressed like one of these. [30]If that is how God clothes the grass of the field, which is here today and tomorrow is thrown into the fire, will he not much more clothe you—you of little faith?

In two instances Jesus demonstrated how God can work when people would share what is available. In one instance He fed five thousand and in another four thousand; each with only a few loaves of bread and a few fish. Yet everyone was satisfied before leaving, and His disciples were able to go around and fill up several baskets of leftover breadcrumbs. In speaking of the five thousand and four thousand they were counting only the men present, not the women and children, so the actual crowds were much larger. These stories are found in Matthew 14:15-21, and Matthew 15:29-39.

Jesus healed many with all types of afflictions. He even brought the dead back to life. His first miracle was performed at a wedding feast in Cana in Galilee where her turned water into wine.

Jesus taught by using parables. He taught about the sower of seeds who would get a good harvest when planting in good soil, but only a poor harvest when planting in poor soil. As to weeds, He said not to pull them out now, which could also destroy some good wheat, but to allow the weeds to grow with the wheat. The weeds would be separated out at harvest time. This is similar to how the souls of people would be separated at the harvest time and entry to the Kingdom of Heaven.

One of his most famous parables dealt with one lost sheep. There were a hundred sheep in the flock, and ninety-nine of them were safe and secured, yet the good shepherd went out to find the lost one and bring it in. This, too is how God acts. He seeks to save the lost, and all Heaven rejoices when the lost are found. We can find this story in Matthew 18:10-14.

Jesus had many detractors who would try to trick Him. Sometimes with money and the payment of taxes, and at another time concerning the Ten Commandments. We did not enumerate the ten while describing the Exodus. The commandments are found in Exodus 20 and were given to Moses at Mt. Sinai. We know, however, that the first four dealt with loving God. First was to love God and have no other Gods before Him; second, do not worship idols; and third do not take the Lord's name in vain. The fourth one was a reminder to keep the Sabbath day Holy. The fifth required that we honor our father and mother. Six through ten had to do with our relation to others. Mankind was commanded to commit no murder, nor adultery, nor stealing, nor to give any false testimony, and to not covet anything belonging to others.

When asked which was the greatest Commandment:

[37]Jesus replied: "Love the Lord your God with all your heart and with all your soul and with all your mind. [38]This is the first and greatest commandment. [39]And the second is like it: Love your neighbor as yourself. [40]All the Law and the Prophets hang on these two commandments." See, Matthew 22:37-40.

One of the most fundamental teachings of Jesus was given in a conversation with a Pharisee named Nicodemus. Jesus had told him that no one would enter the kingdom of God without first being "born again." Nicodemus wondered how a grown man could be born again. In John 3: 5-8:

> [5]Jesus answered, "Very truly I tell you, no one can enter the kingdom of God unless they are born of water and the Spirit. [6]Flesh gives birth to flesh, but the Spirit gives birth to spirit. [7]You should not be surprised at my saying, 'You must be born again.' [8]The wind blows wherever it pleases. You hear its sound, but you cannot tell where it comes from or where it is going. So it is with everyone born of the Spirit."

Jesus concluded his conversation with Nicodemus when he said, "[14]Just as Moses lifted up the snake in the wilderness, so the Son of Man must be lifted up, [15]that everyone who believes may have eternal life in him." See John 3:14-15.

We also note that Jesus is predicting his crucifixion when he points out that like Moses who lifted up the snake in the desert the Son of Man will be lifted up and, thereafter, those that believe in Him may have eternal life. For those who may not be aware, the lifted-up serpent is the symbol for the medical profession. It is the symbol of healing. The story of Moses making the bronze serpent and lifting it on a pole in the desert is found in Numbers 21:8-9. Those who had been bitten could look upon it and be healed. Those who would look upon the cross with Jesus could find eternal life.

All that Jesus did and instructed is just too much for this writing. I can only encourage each of you to read the four Gospels, and the Epistles in the New Testament. We will, however, consider some of the teachings and instructions Jesus gave to his disciples just prior to his death.

D. JESUS BEGINS PREPARING HIS DISCIPLES FOR HIS DEATH

Jesus was talking with His disciples just prior to Passover, and in John 12:23-27 we read,

> [23]Jesus replied, "The hour has come for the Son of Man to be glorified. [24]Very truly I tell you, unless a kernel of wheat falls to the ground and dies, it remains only a single seed. But if it dies, it produces many seeds. [25]Anyone who loves their life will lose it, while anyone who hates their life in this world will keep it for eternal life. [26]Whoever serves me must follow me; and where I am, my servant also will be. My Father will honor the one who serves me. [27]"Now my soul is troubled, and what shall I say? 'Father, save me from this hour'? No, it was for this very reason I came to this hour."

While celebrating an early Passover meal Jesus washed the feet of his disciples, prayed with them, and for them and He predicted His betrayal. He also predicted that Peter would deny Him three times. As quoted in John 13:33-35 Jesus also told His disciples:

> [33]"My children, I will be with you only a little longer. You will look for me, and just as I told the Jews, so I tell you now: Where I am going, you cannot come. [34]A new command I give you: Love one another. As I have loved you, so you must love one another. [35]By this everyone will know that you are my disciples, if you love one another.'"

Jesus gave his disciples further comfort when he said:

> "Do not let your hearts be troubled. You believe in God[a]; believe also in me. [2]My Father's house has many rooms; if that were

not so, would I have told you that I am going there to prepare a place for you? ³And if I go and prepare a place for you, I will come back and take you to be with me that you also may be where I am. ⁴You know the way to the place where I am going." See John 14:1-4.

The disciple Thomas was troubled and said, "If we don't know where you are going how do we know the way?" In John 14:6-7 we read, *⁶Jesus answered, "I am the way and the truth and the life. No one comes to the Father except through me. ⁷If you really know me, you will know my* Father as well. From now on, you do know him and have seen him." (Emphasis added)

Jesus promises more concerning the Holy Spirit and in John 14:15-17, He says:

¹⁵"If you love me, keep my commands. ¹⁶And I will ask the Father, and he will give you another advocate to help you and be with you forever—¹⁷*the Spirit of truth.* The world cannot accept him, because it neither sees him nor knows him. *But you know him, for he lives with you and will be in you."* (Emphasis added)

Jesus tells his disciples that He is the vine and they are the branches. They must remain attached to Him to bear fruit. He also advises them that the world hates Him, and they will hate them also. We can see that this applies to Christians today and for tomorrow. The world will persecute the believers. Also, remember that we must remain attached to Jesus as Christians to bear fruit.

Finally, at the last meal with His disciples prior to Passover, Jesus prays for Himself, for His disciples, and for all future believers. This prayer is found in John 17:1-26. In relevant part, it reads:

After Jesus said this, he looked toward heaven and prayed:

"Father, the hour has come. Glorify your Son, that your Son may glorify you. ²For you granted him authority over all people that he might give eternal life to all those you have given him. . . .⁴I have brought you glory on earth by finishing the work you gave me to do. ⁵And now, Father, glorify me in your presence with the glory I had with you before the world began.

JESUS PRAYED THIS PRAYER FOR HIS DISCIPLES

⁶"I have revealed you to those whom you gave me out of the world. They were yours; you gave them to me, and they have obeyed your word . . . ¹¹I will remain in the world no longer, but they are still in the world. ¹²While I was with them, I protected them and kept them safe by that name you gave me. None has been lost except the one doomed to destruction so that Scripture would be fulfilled. (My emphasis. Here, Jesus is referring to the coming betrayal by Judas) . . .¹⁴I have given them your word and the world has hated them, for they are not of the world any more than I am of the world. ¹⁵My prayer is not that you take them out of the world but that you protect them from the evil one. ¹⁶They are not of the world, even as I am not of it. ¹⁷Sanctify them by the truth; your word is truth. ¹⁸As you sent me into the world, I have sent them into the world. ¹⁹For them I sanctify myself, that they too may be truly sanctified.

JESUS PRAYS FOR ALL BELIEVERS WHO HAVE NOT BEEN WITH HIM, NOR SEEN HIM.

²⁰"My prayer is not for them alone. *(The disciples)*. I pray also for those who will believe in me through their message, ²¹that all of them may be one, Father, just as you are in me and I am in you. May they also be in us so that the world may believe that you have sent me. . . . ²⁴"Father, I want those you have given

me to be with me where I am, and to see my glory, the glory you have given me because you loved me before the creation of the world. ²⁵"Righteous Father, though the world does not know you, I know you, and they know that you have sent me. ²⁶I have made you known to them, and will continue to make you known in order that the love you have for me may be in them and that I myself may be in them."

E. JESUS FULFILLS THE LAW PERTAINING TO PASSOVER, UNLEAVENED BREAD, AND FIRST FRUITS, AND HE CREATES THE NEW COVENANT

¹⁷*"Do not think that I have come to abolish the Law or the Prophets; I have not come to abolish them but to fulfill them.* ¹⁸For truly I tell you, until heaven and earth disappear, not the smallest letter, not the least stroke of a pen, will by any means disappear from the Law until everything is accomplished." (Emphasis mine). See Matthew 5:17-18.

Indeed, Jesus did fulfill the law and the prophets and in this section we will specifically be addressing how He fulfilled the law concerning the three feasts of Unleavened Bread, Passover, and First Fruits.

Annually, Jesus, first with his family, and later with disciples, traveled to Jerusalem for each of the convocations. It might be noted that at the time of Jesus Jerusalem had a population of about 60,000 people. During the convocations the population would swell to approximately 250,000. Even if these numbers are not exactly correct, the point is that the population swelled at the time of the three annual convocations.

Exodus 12 was fairly clear on the requirements for Passover with selecting the lamb on the tenth day of the first month, inspecting it for three days, slaughtering it on the fourteenth day at twilight, roasting it, and then eating it and celebrating the feast of Passover on the fifteenth day of the first month. While the requirement for the feast of Unleavened Bread was also part of the Passover, it was not as clear as sacrificing the lamb, using its blood to mark the homes, and eating the lamb. Therefore, before showing exactly how Jesus fulfilled every dot and tittle of the requirements of Passover, Unleavened Bread, and First Fruits, I will give an explanation about the feasts as well as an explanation of the Jewish calendar which is significant in understanding all of the details.

Unleavened Bread is the main portion of the first memorial convocation and threefold feast. The feast of Unleavened Bread continued for seven days. Within the convocation was also the feast of First Fruits, which was observed on "the morrow" or the day after the Jewish Sabbath. The Jewish Sabbath was from sundown on what we refer to as Friday in the common calendar, until sunset on what we refer to as Saturday. The morrow would, therefore, begin at sundown on Saturday and go through sunset on the day we refer to as Sunday. For this reason, resurrection day or Easter will always fall on Sunday, no matter what day of the week Passover is observed or the feast of Unleavened Bread begins.

In natural Israel, Passover and Unleavened Bread were required in Exodus 12. Symbolically, we might say that Passover got the Israelites out of Egypt, and Unleavened Bread got Egypt out of the Israelites. (I recall hearing that expression on a tape by Rick Godwin, and I find it to be most fitting.) First Fruits was not mentioned nor prescribed until after the Israelites had safely passed through the waters and out of Egypt. This feast was required after they entered the Promised Land, and when they could have their own crops. The three convocations were to be held according to the Jewish religious calendar in the first month with the three feasts, the third month with Pentecost or Feast of Harvest, and in the seventh month the three feasts of Trumpets, The Day of Atonement, and Tabernacles.

In Exodus 12:14-17, we read,

"¹⁴This is a day you are to commemorate; for the generations to come you shall celebrate it as a festival to the Lord—a lasting ordinance. ¹⁵For seven days you are to eat bread made without yeast. On the first day remove the yeast from your houses, for whoever eats anything with yeast in it from the first day through the seventh must be cut off from Israel. ¹⁶On the first day hold a sacred assembly, and another one on the seventh day. Do no work at all on these days, except to prepare food for everyone to eat; that is all you may do. ¹⁷"Celebrate the Festival of Unleavened Bread, because it was on this very day that I brought your divisions out of Egypt. Celebrate this day as a lasting ordinance for the generations to come."

There is nothing bad or wrong about leaven. It is simply yeast. It is used regularly in cooking and making our food tastier or lighter. Symbolically, however, it is different. It puffs things up, and a little leaven will puff up the whole loaf. It works silently from the inside out. Leaven spiritually symbolizes evil. The Israelites were told to "get it out." If there is anything defiling your home or your church, get it out. On the positive side, it was a remembrance that God took the Israelites out of Egypt. (Or, God got Egypt out of the Israelites.)

There are at least five types of "leaven" mentioned in the New Testament. In Matthew 16:6-12, Jesus identifies the leaven of the Pharisees and that of the Sadducees. The leaven of the Pharisees was hypocrisy, and the leaven of the Sadducees was a denial of the supernatural and miracles. See also Luke 12:1, and Mark 12:18. We are also told of the leaven the Herodians, which is worldliness or love of the world. See Mark 8:15 and 1 John 2:15. Another type of leaven was that of the Galatians, which was the love of the law. They sought to be justified by legalisms and works which kept them in bondage to the law. They were concerned about the little things that provided an outward showing. Paul referred to them as "foolish." See Galatians 3.

The Apostle Paul identifies a fifth type of leaven which was that of the Corinthians. This was malice, wickedness, sins of the flesh, and sexual immorality. In 1 Corinthians 5, Paul told the Corinthians to remove one their members before the whole group became corrupted. However, in 2 Corinthians 7, Paul rejoiced for the repentance of that individual, and urged his acceptance back into the group. A passage which will be familiar to most Christians is found in 1 Corinthians 5:7-8. It reads:

"7Get rid of the old yeast, so that you may be a new unleavened batch—as you really are. *For Christ, our Passover lamb, has been sacrificed. 8Therefore let us keep the Festival, not with the old bread leavened with malice and wickedness, but with the unleavened bread of sincerity and truth.*" (Emphasis added)

We can see that Paul is also identifying Christ as the Passover Lamb of God, and the significance of leaven.

In keeping the feast, we put away "leaven." We must set aside our leaven whatever that might be, to be sanctified for Christ. Jesus came to forgive and to atone for our sin. Sin is destroyed by the power of the Cross and the shedding of His Blood. Sin happens, but the Holy Spirit convicts us when we do wrong, and by repenting we are forgiven. When we accept Jesus and are justified by our belief, in Him, we must immediately put out the leaven, repent, and be determined to keep the leaven out.

We keep the Feast of Unleavened Bread these days in the church through communion and eating the bread. Spiritually, Jesus is the bread of life. He was unleavened and without sin. He had none of the characteristics we have used to illustrate "leaven." In 1 Corinthians 10:14-17, we find:

14Therefore, my dear friends, flee from idolatry. 15I speak to sensible people; judge for yourselves what I say. 16Is not the cup of thanksgiving for which we give thanks a participation in the blood of Christ? And is not the bread that we break a participation in the body of Christ? [17]Because there is one loaf, we, who are many, are one body, for we all share the one loaf.

Jesus also reminded all to get the leaven out. In Luke 17:32 he said, "remember Lots wife." As she was leaving Sodom, she simply had to look back. She just couldn't put it all aside and was not allowed to go farther. She was turned into a pillar of salt.

We keep the Feast of Unleavened Bread by feeding on the unleavened Jesus and fellowship with others and in the fellowship with Christ. Some Church denominations provide communion daily, some weekly, and others less frequently. Some, one might say, rarely. Personally, I receive a spiritual uplift when I "feed" on Jesus, and remember the sacrifice He made for me, so I prefer having it observed fairly frequently.

I have observed that there is a limited understanding of most of these feasts, but perhaps First Fruits in particular. You may wonder what is "First Fruits," why is it required, and what does it represent symbolically. In Leviticus 23:9-11 we read,

"[9]The Lord said to Moses, [10]"Speak to the Israelites and say to them: 'When you enter the land I am going to give you and you reap its harvest, bring to the priest a sheaf of the first grain you harvest. [11]He is to wave the sheaf before the Lord so it will be accepted on your behalf; the priest is to wave it on the day after the Sabbath."

When the Israelites began to have their own crops, and the wheat or barley began to grow, they were to collect a "sheaf" and bring it to the priest to be waved before the Lord and found to be acceptable. This also was to ensure the success of the crop and the rest of the harvest. It was the "first" of the "fruits."

In the Old Testament, a "sheaf" also represented a person. Remember earlier when we referred to Joseph's dream which caused his brothers to despise him and sell him. We learned that while they were binding sheaves of grain in the field, the sheaf of Joseph rose and stood upright while the sheaves gathered around him bowed to him. The symbolism also applies in the New Testament to the person of Jesus Christ who presented Himself to the Father while fulfilling the Feast of First Fruits. We learn in John 20:16-17 that:

> "¹⁶Jesus said to her, "Mary." She turned toward him and cried out in Aramaic, "Rabboni!" (Which means teacher).
>
> ¹⁷Jesus said, "Do not hold on to me, for I have not yet ascended to the Father. Go instead to my brothers and tell them, 'I am ascending to my Father and your Father, to my God and your God.'"

Why would Jesus tell Mary not to touch Him? The fact is He was ascending to the Father to be presented as the sheaf and wave offering and to be found suitable. At a later time, he had no problem in allowing His disciples to touch Him, and specifically He invited Thomas to put his finger in the holes in His hands and in His side where the spear had pierced Him.

We also have the Apostle Paul's interpretation of these events. In 1 Corinthians 15:20-23 we learn:

> "²⁰But Christ has indeed been raised from the dead, the first fruits of those who have fallen asleep. ²¹For since death came through a man, the resurrection of the dead comes also through a man. ²²*For as in Adam all die, so in Christ all will be made alive.*

²³*But each in turn: Christ, the first fruits;* then, when he comes, those who belong to him." (Emphasis added.)

We can note from that passage that we may all be part of the harvest of souls, the crop of those "who belong to Him." While thinking about this situation, remember that you must believe and accept Him as your Savior. You must take the "gift" He offers. Publicly express your acceptance of this gift if you have not done so. The risk of not accepting His gift is just too great.

Allow me to digress a bit at this point and explain some things you should know about the Jewish calendar, and how they keep time. The Jews used two calendars, a religious and a civil. The civil calendar has twelve months, all based on the moon, so occasionally an extra month is added. (About every nineteen years). This keeps this first month of the religious calendar in the spring. Passover, First Fruits, and Unleavened Bread will always be celebrated in the month of March or April.

Some months have 30 days, but others have 29 with an overall average of approximately 29.5 days. The *first month of the religious calendar* begins with Nissan (although sometimes known as Abid). The months always begin with a new moon. In relation to the common calendar, the first day of Nissan in 2015* began on March 21, a Saturday. Although for the Jews, it actually began at sundown on Friday the 20ᵗʰ. (Incidentally, the common year of 2015, coincides with the year 5776 in the Jewish civil calendar). The tenth day of Nissan, the day the lambs would be taken or selected, fell on a Monday, March 30. Five days later, or the 15ᵗʰ of Nissan, Passover came. It was on Saturday, April 4. Again, however, in actuality, Passover began at sundown on Friday, April 3. Easter and First Fruits fell on Sunday, April 5, or in 2015, Nissan 16. (See, exhibit A, page 102, for the days and timing in the year Jesus died and was resurrected.)

---

* 2015 was the year the first edition of this book was published.

I realize this is confusing, but it is important to understand. Remember that the Jewish day begins with a night half starting at sundown, while our days begin at midnight. A feast day will begin with the night half, with the actual celebration beginning at sundown, as with Passover and the beginning of Unleavened Bread. However, with other celebrations, they will be mainly observed in the following day half during daylight hours.

The month of Lyar follows Nissan and it has 29 days. The third month of the Jewish religious calendar is Sivan and, in this year, 2015, the feast of Pentecost fell on Monday, May 25, although it began Sunday, the 24th, at sundown. Pentecost is also known as the Feast of Harvest or Feast of Weeks. They are all the same thing, just a different name. It is a time for the early corn, barley, or wheat harvest. It is 7 weeks and a day following the Feast of First Fruits for a total 50 days, thus "Pentecost."

Although I will skip the other names of months in the Jewish calendar, I will mention that the last day of the Jewish civil year is Elul 29. In 2015 this ended on Sunday September 13, at sundown. *The Jewish New Year under the civil calendar* begins at sundown on the 13th but is celebrated on the day half of the 14th which is Tishrei 1. The Jewish New Year is known as Rosh Hashanah.

This year has been the seventh or Sabbath year (Shemitah), and at the end of Elul 29, September 13, all debts are to be forgiven. Tishrei 1 will also be the beginning of a year of Jubilee which falls after the seventh Sabbath of years. I will not make any predictions, but very frequently, these days and periods have a noticeable significance in worldly affairs and finances. Remember 2001 and 2008. Now we are at seven years later. It is 2015.

Tishrei 1 is also *the first day of the seventh month of the religious calendar* and is the day for celebrating the Feast of Trumpets. This is the beginning of another commemoration which has three feasts. On the tenth day of the month is the most Holy day for the Jewish people. It is the Day of Atonement, also known as Yom Kippur. This year it will begin at sundown on Tuesday, September 22.

The big fall convocation is the full moon harvest festival known as Tabernacles, which will begin at sundown on September 27. Tabernacles is a feast celebrating the final in-gathering of the harvest with the wine and oil and all that has been produced for the year. The Feast of Tabernacles runs for seven days and always begins on the fifteenth day of Tishrei with the full moon. It is also known as the festival of booths, celebrating the time when the Israelites lived in booths.

In the Church, today, we have experienced Passover, Unleavened Bread, First Fruits and Pentecost, each being completely fulfilled. However, the fulfillment of Tabernacles is yet to come. It will be the big one, and at the end of the age, or at preparation for the return of Jesus Christ. Perhaps we should start listening for the "trumpets."

By now, the Jewish timing of days and hours should be fairly discernable. The Jewish day is divided into a night half and a day half with the night half coming first. It begins at sundown and runs until sunrise. The day half runs from sunrise to sunset. During the spring and autumn, which correspond to Passover and Tabernacles, each half would be generally 6:00 p.m. to 6:00 a.m. and from 6:00 a.m. to 6:00 p.m. During the day half, the third hour would be equivalent of 9:00 a.m. The sixth hour would be noon, and ninth hour would be 3:00 p.m. or twilight.

F. THE ULTIMATE SACRIFICE

Jesus knew He came to create a New Blood Covenant between Himself and God, the Father, for the benefit of all mankind. He was to be the perfect Lamb of God, the sacrificial lamb. He knew He would die, and that on the third day He would be resurrected. In Matthew 12:40, Jesus is quoted: "*40 For as Jonah was three days and three nights* in the belly of a huge fish, so *the Son of Man will be three days and three nights in the heart of the earth.*" (Emphasis added)

Concerning a determination of when Jesus actually died and how long he would remain in His grave, I should mention two things. One is that the Jews would consider any part of a day as a day, and also that the other Gospels merely mention that Jesus would be dead for three days. In that sense, one could say that by dying at 3:00 p.m. Friday the three hours from then until sundown was one day. The time from sundown on Friday until sunset on Saturday was a second day, and then from sunset on Saturday until sometime before sunrise on Sunday, would constitute the third day. However, I believe what Jesus Himself said is correct. If so, He would have had to die on Thursday afternoon at twilight and then you would have at least parts of three days and three nights prior to resurrection. It also makes more sense to me when we count the hours for either belief. If He died on what is commonly referred to Good Friday, He would been buried for no more than thirty-nine hours. But if he was crucified on Thursday, He would have been dead and buried for approximately sixty-three hours. You can do the math by figuring from 3:00 p.m. on the date of death until 6:00 am on the day of resurrection.

Also, in determining the timing of the events during the year in which Jesus died, we can see that if he entered Jerusalem on the tenth day of the first month, the day the people selected their lamb, and if that was on a Sunday, which we celebrate as Palm Sunday, then there is no way the death of Jesus would happen on Friday. Palm Sunday and Good Friday simply do not add up together.

In John 12:1 we are told that six days before Passover, Jesus came to Bethany where Lazarus lived, whom Jesus had raised from the dead. Six days before Passover would be the ninth day of Nissan. John 12:12 tells us: "The next day the great crowd that had come to the festival heard that Jesus was on His way to Jerusalem, and they celebrated His arrival." The next day would be the tenth, the day the lambs were selected. There is a "sheep gate" which some theologians "speculate" Jesus might have used when entering Jerusalem.

From the writings in the Gospels, we learn that Jesus was questioned and challenged by the Pharisees, Sadducees, and others until the fourteenth. Jesus was causing trouble for the Temple hierarchy, and they wanted Him dead. They were fearful that the crowds might get out of control, and the Romans might have to shut down the Passover celebration.

During this three-day period, Jesus also threw the money changers out of the Temple. The Temple had its own currency, and in order for those who did not bring their own sacrifices, and had to buy something to sacrifice, they would have to change what money they had into the Temple money. The money changers were, indeed, a bunch of thieves. Jesus did stir things up during this brief time.

He celebrated an early Passover meal with his disciples. Keep in mind, however, that as to a Jewish day, the fourteenth began at sundown on what we would call Wednesday, during this specific week in the year in which he died. The fourteenth would run until sundown the following day, which would be what we call Thursday, and by the afternoon of the fourteenth He had been tried and crucified.

It was during this early celebration that Jesus took unleavened bread and the wine and announced the New Covenant, which would be made with the sacrifice of His body and blood. He told His disciples that whenever they did this in the future to do it in remembrance of Him. When it is celebrated, it must be done with a clean heart and a right spirit. (Read Matthew 26:26-29; Mark 14:22-25; Luke 22:19-22; and 1 Corinthians 11:23-29)

Judas left the meal and went to tell the high priest of Jesus's whereabouts. Following the meal Jesus and His disciples went to Gethsemane to pray, and while there, Jesus was arrested. He was taken to the high priest for questioning and to King Herod and to Pilate, the Roman Governor. He was found innocent by both. He was still the unblemished Lamb.

The Temple officials wanted Jesus executed, but did not have the power to do it, so they continued insisting that Pilate issue the order. In the end, although he attempted to "wash his hands" of it, he ordered flogging and crucifixion. The Gospels tell of the crowd yelling "crucify

Him," but I wonder just who made up that "crowd." It was in a reasonably confined area, near the Temple, and the masses, who adored Jesus were generally camped outside the city walls. In all likelihood, it was mostly the Temple crowd, or "gang."

It was on the fourteenth at about the sixth hour, noon, that Jesus was finally put on the cross at Calvary. In John 19:14 we read, "¹⁴It was the day of Preparation of the Passover; it was about noon . . ." Jesus had bled from the crown of thorns and the scourging he had received from the Roman soldiers. Most people would have died from all that he had suffered, yet they continued by nailing His hands, or wrists, and His feet to the cross. We are told that the sky grew dark, and Jesus hung on the cross until about the ninth hour (3:00 p.m.). This would be the same approximate time the kosher four-legged lambs were slaughtered.

In John 19:28-30 we read,

> ²⁸Later, knowing that everything had now been finished, and so that Scripture would be fulfilled, Jesus said, "I am thirsty." ²⁹A jar of wine vinegar was there, so they soaked a sponge in it, put the sponge on a stalk of the hyssop plant, and lifted it to Jesus' lips. ³⁰When he had received the drink, Jesus said, "*It is finished.*" With that, he bowed his head and gave up his spirit. (Emphasis added)

Other Gospels give other last words, such as "Father forgive them for they know not what they do," and "Into your hands I commit my spirit." He might have uttered all of these expressions; however, I find that the words "it is finished" have special significance. In one of the tapes by either Smith or Godwin, I learned that the term also meant "we've won." It would be what the commander of an army would announce to mean we have victory, we have won. This, too, might be why the Centurion standing at the cross was able to conclude that, truly this was the son of God.

The Gospels tell us that other things happened at the time of Jesus's death. The heavy veil of the temple, setting apart the Holy of Holies, was split from the top to the bottom. This would symbolize that there is now a way to the Father other than through the Jewish high priest. There was a great earthquake.

Several prophesies were fulfilled at this time. No bones were broken. It was a custom to break the bones of those crucified so that they would die more quickly. This did not happen to Jesus as He had already died even before they put the spear in His side, which fulfilled yet another prophesy. A third prophesy being fulfilled at the time of His death was that they cast lots for his clothing. When we consider all this prophesy, or history before it happened, things like this cannot be made up.

Jesus's body was prepared for burial and then placed in a new and nearby tomb. This honor would have been unheard of for a common criminal and anyone who had been crucified. Nevertheless, in John 19:41-42 we read, "⁴¹At the place where Jesus was crucified, there was a garden, and in the garden a new tomb, in which no one had ever been laid. ⁴²Because it was the Jewish day of Preparation and since the tomb was nearby, they laid Jesus there."

All of this had to be done prior to sundown, because the day of Passover was about to begin. Like a Sabbath, Passover is a Holy Day when no work could be done.

For a comparison of Passover with Holy Week in the year Jesus died see **Exhibit A**. The exhibit shows that Jesus entered Jerusalem on the tenth day of Nissan, which was a Sunday by our common calendar. It shows that he died around the ninth hour, or 3:00 pm on the fourteenth, which would be a Thursday. His resurrection occurred on the seventeenth of Nissan, or a Sunday. First Fruits, or Easter, or Resurrection Day will always fall on a Sunday. It occurs on the "morrow" after the Jewish Sabbath, no matter what day of the week the Feasts of Passover and Unleavened Bread might begin.

Exhibit A. Timing of the events of Holy Week in the year Jesus was crucified.

	9th SATURDAY	10th SUNDAY	11th MONDAY	12th TUESDAY	13th WEDNESDAY
	Jesus in Bethany Sundown, the 10th begins	Jesus enters Jerusalem Passover lambs selected	Jesus in and around Jerusalem Passover lambs inspected for defects, and kept until the 14th	Jesus questioned and inspected	Jesus arranges early Passover with disciples
	Saturday	At midnight, Sunday begins	At midnight, the successive days of Mon., Tue., & Wed. begin		

The 14th was the day of preparation for Passover and Unleavened Bread. It began at sundown and had so many events, we will use one entire line to cover that day. In our calendar, it would be Thursday, beginning at midnight.

6:00 p.m. to Midnight	Midnight to 6:00 a.m.	6:00 a.m. to 9:00 a.m. (3rd hour)	9:00 a.m. to noon (6th hour)	3:00 p.m. (9th hour)	to Sundown or 6:00 p.m.
Early Passover meal Jesus announces New Covenant.	Jesus arrested Questioned Found innocent by Herod and Pilate	Jesus sentenced Mocked Beaten	Taken to the Cross Darkness	Jesus dies "It is finished" New Covenant established	Jesus placed in Tomb Temple veil torn Passover began at sundown

15th Friday	16th Saturday		17th Sunday	
Jesus in the tomb Jewish Sabbath began at sundown.	Jesus in the tomb Jewish Sabbath until sundown		The morrow; 1st day of week; Jesus resurrected before dawn	
Friday began at midnight.	Saturday began at midnight.		Sunday begins at midnight.	

Although earlier attempts were made to kill Jesus, we learn in John 7:30: "his time had not yet come." The plan was fixed by God for Jesus to die at the time the Passover lambs were being slaughtered.

Several years ago, I cut an article out of my local newspaper. Unfortunately, I do not find the date of publication. However, it was an article by the Associated Press with a location of London, and entitled, "Scientists pinpoint date of Crucifixion as April 3, 33 A.D." The names of the scientists are Colin J. Humphreys and W. G. Waddington, both of Oxford University. Their article had been published in the British magazine *Nature*. The conclusion was based on such evidence as the time of ten years in which Pilate was the Roman procurator in Judea, when a solar eclipse occurred, and the timing of a full moon which would have coincided with Passover. (FYI: Passover and Tabernacles will always coincide with a full moon.) They also refer to a lunar eclipse, or blood moon. (FYI: We also witnessed a blood moon on Passover this year and will have another in September at Tabernacles.) Throughout the article, the scientists indicated that April 3 fell on a Friday.

To say the least, the article was interesting. I have no problem with a particular numbered day or year, but I will stand by my analysis that Jesus actually died on what we would call a Thursday afternoon. It would have been the fourteenth of Nissan in the year in which He died. The sky could have grown dark from heavy storm clouds, a dust storm, or whatever, but it is not likely that there was a lunar eclipse and a blood moon on the same day. The moon was full on the day of Passover, Nissan 15, which could have produced a blood moon late in the night, but the moon would have been on the wrong side of the earth to have created a solar eclipse on the same date.

Passover might have been on the common calendar as a Friday, and April 3, could have been the correct date for AD 33. However, Passover began six hours before our Friday began, and since Jesus died about three hours before Passover began, it was on a Thursday afternoon by our common calendar, and it was on Nissan 14 by the Jewish calendar. It should have been understood by the scientists that Passover is the equivalent of the Jewish Sabbath, so in that sense they had two Sabbaths in a row. Passover started at sundown on Thursday, and the Jewish Sabbath started at sundown on what we call Friday. I will stand by my analysis in Exhibit A.

G. THE RESURRECTION

Some of what will be in this section will be a repeat of points that were made earlier, but the repetition is needed.

In John 20:1 we read, "²⁰Early on the first day of the week, while it was still dark, Mary Magdalene went to the tomb and saw that the stone had been removed from the entrance." From this we learn that the resurrection was on the first day of the week which is what we refer to as Sunday. It was "the morrow" after the Jewish Sabbath. It was still dark, so it was before the night half ended and the day half started. It was during the first half of Nissan 17.

Mary told Peter and the disciples that the tomb was empty, and they went and saw the empty tomb. It is noted in John 20:6-7:

⁶Then Simon Peter, who was behind him, arrived and went into the tomb. He saw the strips of linen lying there, ⁷as well as the burial cloth that had been around Jesus' head. *The cloth was folded up by itself, separate from the linen.* (Emphasis added).

It is my understanding that symbolically when the napkin is folded and left behind as the head covering was, it meant "I shall return."

Mary returned to the tomb and was asked why she was crying. She said that they had "taken my Lord away and I don't know where they have put Him." When she turned around, she saw Jesus standing there, but did not yet realize that it was Jesus until He spoke. She had thought it was the gardener. However, it was then that Jesus told her not to touch Him at that time as He had not yet been presented to the Father. We covered that in the part about "first fruits."

As further proof of the resurrection Jesus was seen by His disciples, and by many in several places and at different times. He visited with the ones he met on the road to Emmaus, and according to the Apostle Paul, Jesus was seen by over five hundred at one time and that counted only the men.

Jesus fulfilled the requirements of "unleavened bread" by just being unleavened; not puffed up, and not guilty of the leaven of such as the Pharisees, Sadducees, Herodians, Corinthians, or Galatians.

As noted before, Paul also referred to Jesus Christ as the "Passover lamb" which had been sacrificed and that we were to keep the feast not with the old leaven with malice and wickedness, but with unleavened bread of sincerity and truth. He also noted in 1 Corinthians 15:20: "[20]But Christ has indeed been raised from the dead, the first fruits of those who have fallen asleep."

Jesus had undoubtedly fulfilled every requirement of these three feasts and completed and fulfilled His mission.

Jesus remained on earth for forty days, and then ascended to Heaven, but announced that the Spirit would soon come. Ten days later the Holy Spirit did come, the feast of Pentecost was fulfilled, and the Christian church began.

✝

CHAPTER 6

THE HOLY SPIRIT

"¹When the day of Pentecost came, they were all together in one place. ²Suddenly, a sound like the blowing of a violent wind came from heaven and filled the whole house where they were sitting. ³They saw what seemed to be tongues of fire that separated and came to rest on each of them."

ACT 2: 1-3

This sounds much like the way the Spirit of God came to the Israelites when they were at Sinai. In chapter 4 we concluded that the giving of the law came at Sinai, and that they had arrived roughly fifty days after leaving Egypt. God thereafter ordained that they would commemorate the Feast of Weeks or Harvest, or what we now refer to as Pentecost, fifty days after the Feast of First Fruits. Jesus had been with the disciples for forty days before ascending to Heaven, and in Acts 1:4-5 we learn that: ⁴On one occasion, while he was eating with them, he gave them this command: "Do not leave Jerusalem, but wait for the gift my Father promised, which you have heard me speak about. ⁵For John baptized with water, but in a few days you will be baptized with the Holy Spirit."

Ten days later was the day for the Feast of Pentecost, and the Spirit indeed, came to Jerusalem.

In Acts 2 we are also told that those gathered were filled with the Holy Spirit and began to speak in other tongues. As it was the Feast of Pentecost there were many God-fearing Jews from every nation gathered in that area. In Acts 2:6-12 we find:

⁶When they heard this sound, a crowd came together in bewilderment, because each one heard their own language being spoken. ⁷Utterly amazed, they asked: "Aren't all these who are speaking Galileans? ⁸Then how is it that each of us hears them in our native language? ⁹Parthians, Medes and Elamites; residents of Mesopotamia, Judea and Cappadocia, Pontus and Asia, ¹⁰Phrygia and Pamphylia, Egypt and the parts of Libya near Cyrene; visitors from Rome ¹¹(both Jews and converts to Judaism); Cretans and Arabs—we hear them declaring the wonders of God in our own tongues!" ¹²Amazed and perplexed, they asked one another, "What does this mean?"

Several thought the people had too much to drink. However, Peter, who was himself filled with the Spirit, addressed the crowd and gave them the story of Jesus. Following the teaching by Peter we learn: "⁴¹Those who accepted his message were baptized, and about three thousand were added to their number that day." Acts 2:41. We know that in counting numbers they only counted the men, so more than likely there were as many as 6,000 that were converted that day. That was the beginning of The Church.

The book of Acts covers many actions of the apostles. Led by the Holy Spirit, they performed miracles and signs and wonders. They worked in Jerusalem, and in all Judea, and began moving out to other parts of the known world on missions. Churches were established in many places.

We know from the Holy Bible that the Holy Spirit was not new on the day of Pentecost. The Holy Spirit was with and part of God from the very beginning. In Genesis 1:2 we read, "²Now the earth was formless and empty, darkness was over the surface of the deep, and the *Spirit of God* was hovering over the waters." (Emphasis added) From reading the Old Testament, we know that the Holy Spirit has manifested itself to mankind as God in us. We know also that the Spirit was with Abraham, Moses, and David.

Following David's adulterous activity with Bathsheba, the prophet Nathan came to him and convicted him of the offense. David then wrote Psalm 51, and while I would urge you to read it in its entirety, I will quote only verses 10 and 11: "¹⁰Create in me a pure heart, O God, and renew a steadfast spirit within me. ¹¹*Do not* cast me from your presence or *take your Holy Spirit from me*." (Emphasis added) David was empowered by the Holy Spirit and he knew that he could not afford to lose that source.

We learned from the Prophet Jeremiah, as mentioned in chapter 4, that unlike the law given to Moses in the Ten Commandments, in the days to come, the Holy Spirit would write the law on our hearts. The Holy Spirit is our conscience and sense of ought, but the Holy Spirit also brings power.

A. MANIFESTATIONS OF THE SPIRIT

"¹Now about the gifts of the Spirit, brothers and sisters, I do not want you to be uninformed." 1 Corinthians 12:1

With the indwelling Holy Spirit, we experience God in our lives. God's power is shown by the gifts of the Spirit, while His character is revealed through the fruit of the spirit. The difference between gifts and fruits was discussed in an earlier chapter. The gift of faith can be both a gift and a fruit. The new believer comes to Christ through the gift of faith, but as the believer matures, that faith develops more like a fruit.

In 1 Corinthians 12:8-10 we learn that there are nine gifts. Dr. Parish, the lecturer at the Bible study mentioned in the Preface as a source for much of my knowledge concerning the Holy Spirit, divided the gifts into three general groups. There are gifts that reveal something, such as a word of wisdom, a word of knowledge, and the discerning of spirits. There are also gifts of power which would include the gift of faith, the gift of healing, and the working of miracles. A third group includes those gifts which are spoken, such as prophesy, the speaking in tongues, and the interpretation of tongues.

Although there are several gifts, there is but one Spirit which gives those diverse gifts. See 1 Corinthians 12:4. There are also differences of administrations but the same Lord. See 1 Corinthians 12:5. There is one Jesus Christ the head of the Church, but five ministries are revealed. There will be apostles, prophets, evangelists, pastors, and some will be teachers. See Ephesians 4:11. Each of the ministries has a unified purpose which would be the edification of the Church, the body of Christ. Ephesians 4:12. The Church today needs the power of the Holy Spirit more and more. There is no way to accomplish the work of God through mere manpower of the flesh. The anointing by the Holy Spirit is probably needed more today than even on the day of Pentecost and the condition of the Church in the first century. God will manifest the gifts of the Spirit through individuals who will yield themselves to God. That includes YOU!

Come Lord Jesus. Come Holy Spirit. Fill the hearts of your faithful.

The gifts of the Spirit referred to in 1 Corinthians is not the "Spirit of wisdom" or knowledge which was given to Jesus, but a fragment or a word which is to meet a need that exists at a specified time. The word of wisdom is closely related to the word of knowledge and to the discerning of spirits. We must be careful when discerning where a word of wisdom or knowledge comes from. It could from the devil, which could bring trouble, or it could be mere human wisdom. Human wisdom can sometimes be a problem when selecting Church leaders. One might assume that because someone is shrewd in business affairs that he or she could be a successful leader for the Church. God does not need man's shrewdness. It can sometimes cause havoc.

In 1 Corinthians 1:19-20 we read, "19For it is written: "I will destroy the wisdom of the wise. . . . 20Where is the wise person? Where is the teacher of the law? Where is the philosopher of this age? Has not God made foolish the wisdom of the world?"

There can be counterfeits of wisdom and knowledge. If one is involved with the occult, that knowledge will likely be satanic and should be avoided like the plague. Such may come from ESP or fortune tellers. Why would anyone seek knowledge or wisdom from such a source? Satan is a known liar and not trustworthy.

We find a good example of divine wisdom in James 3:17, which reads: "17But the wisdom that comes from heaven is first of all pure; then peace-loving, considerate, submissive, full of mercy and good fruit, impartial and sincere."

Concerning the word of knowledge, it, too is a fragment. The Spirit is able to give a word of knowledge that is needed at a particular time. It is not the same as learned knowledge, but it is knowledge that you had no other way of knowing. A good biblical example of the working of a word knowledge can be found in the conversion of Saul, who became the Apostle Paul. Paul had been blinded on the road to Damascus and was led into the city. God had spoken to a man named Ananias and told him to go to a certain place where he would meet Saul. Ananias had no way of knowing any of this, but his obedience led to the conversion of the Apostle Paul. See Acts 9:10-18.

When it comes to the gift of discerning of spirits, we are not talking about a gift of "discernment," which could likely come from mere suspicion. Such has nothing to do with God. A true discerning of spirits can tell what kind of spirit is present, whether it comes from God, something demonic, or is merely human.

When I contemplate the three gifts of wisdom, knowledge, and discerning, two outside sources come to mind. Years ago when I was a vestryman at the Grace Episcopal Church in Paducah, Kentucky, the Vestry learned about the leadership of Father Everett "Terry" Fullam at St. Paul's Parish in Darien, Connecticut. At that time, he had one of the fastest-growing parishes in the United States. A book entitled *Miracle in Darien* was written about Fullam by Bob Slosser.[1] One of the credits given to Father Fullam in his leadership of the vestry was that there would be no "devil's advocates." Any decision which was to be followed had to be by unanimous consent. That method is surely not to say no suggestion can be challenged or debated, but the final decision in his parish had to be unanimous. Whatever, it seemed to work very well.

My thoughts also turned to a work by C.S. Lewis entitled *The Screwtape Letters*.[2] I find a lot of truth and humor in them. There are thirty-one of these letters written from the Senior Demon Screwtape to his nephew Wormwood, one of the junior tempters. Screwtape advises Wormwood how to carry out his responsibility of securing the damnation of a man who is known as "patient." While the letters are fiction, the plot and characters do address Christian theological issues. Screwtape works in the "lowerarchy" of hell. His advice to Wormwood helps to undermine human faith and promote sin. Reading these letters will certainly make us aware of our own human nature and shortcomings. Apparently, neither of the demons was capable of comprehending God's love or human virtue.

The gifts of faith, healings, and miracles are closely related. However, the gift of faith seems to be fairly clear. "Now faith is confidence in what we hope for and assurance about what we do not see." Hebrews 11:1. Faith is now, and hope is in the future. We have faith in Jesus Christ, and our hope is for eternal salvation.

I believe that faith that counts for anything is faith that works. We are told that we are saved by faith and not by works lest we could boast.

However, we learn in James 2:17: "¹⁷In the same way, faith by itself, if it is not accompanied by action, is dead." So, to put all of this another way, a person is not saved by works, but he is saved by faith that works. Get on the team. Do something to show your faith and love of God. Spread the word and bring others to salvation. Show up.

You might think that you know Jesus, but does He know who you are? Consider the story of the ten virgins. In Matthew 25: 1-13 we find the whole message, but in verses 10-12, we read, "¹⁰But while they were on their way to buy the oil, the bridegroom arrived. The virgins who were ready went in with him to the wedding banquet. And the door was shut. ¹¹Later the others also came. "Lord, Lord," they said, "open the door for us!"¹² *But he replied, "Truly I tell you, I don't know you."* (Emphasis added.)

Let your faith be known.

Our faith is grounded on the word of God, the Bible. We must learn what is in it. We cannot stand on the promises, if we don't know what they are. We read in Romans 10:17: "¹⁷Consequently, faith comes from hearing the message, and the message is heard through the word about Christ." We believe when we know. We believe better, when we not only know, but also understand. Hopefully, the information in this book will help you understand Christianity.

While I am aware of having had the benefit of gifts of a word of knowledge, a word of wisdom, and faith, and perhaps some discerning of spirits, I am not as aware of receiving the gifts of healing and miracles. Perhaps I have, spiritually and physically. In my opinion, however, the gifts of healing and miracles are not in the one who might lay hands on, or who prays for, someone. A person may be involved, but the gift comes from God or the Holy Spirit to the one who receives the healing or miracle.

Healing was certainly a large part of the ministry in the earlier church, and many miracles and healings are described in the Book of the *Acts of the Apostles* and other Epistles. We also have learned of the many healings and miracles performed by Jesus. His entire three years of ministry was one miracle after another. He healed the sick, restored sight to the blind, made the lame walk, made the deaf hear, made the dumb speak, and even raised the dead. He, too, was raised from the dead. As a Christian we must believe these things and not be like the Sadducees which denied miracles and anything supernatural. How were they able to deny such when they were seeing them in plain sight? That is a mystery.

I am not aware that I have received any gift of prophesy, nor have I had the gift of speaking in tongues. However, I have heard many prophesies these days, and I have heard people speaking in tongues, and even someone was present who could make an interpretation.

These latter two gifts seem to be the most controversial. Many claim that the gift of tongues and interpretations have ceased, but it seems that they will not end until the return of Jesus in His second coming. We read in 1 Corinthians 13:9-10: "⁹For we know in part and we prophesy in part, ¹⁰but when completeness comes, what is in part disappears." Reading on in verse 12 we find, "¹²For now we see only a reflection as in a mirror; then we shall see face to face. Now I know in part; then I shall know fully, even as I am fully known." The gifts will not be needed after Christ returns, but there is no reason to believe that they have ceased.

We have these gifts. Let us use them for God's glory. Keep your eyes and ears and your heart open.

B. SANCTIFICATION BY THE HOLY SPIRIT, AND WHAT IT CAN MEAN

We hear about terms such as justification or redemption and sanctification, but what do they mean, and how do they apply? We are justified through Christ by our faith and belief in Him. Justification would be the same as redemption.

We have heard, also that some Christians can produce thirty-fold results, and others sixty-fold. So much more can be accomplished for the Glory of God with sanctification by the Holy Spirit. One of the best explanations of the difference between mere justification and sanctification, and what kind of power can be released in us through the Holy Spirit, was written in a book by Major W. Ian Thomas entitled *The Saving Life of Christ*.[3] On pages 17 and 18 he wrote:

"How stupid it would be to buy a car with a powerful engine under the hood, and then to spend the rest of your days pushing it! Thwarted and exhausted, you would wish to discard it as a useless thing! Yet to some of you who are Christians, this may be God's word to your heart. When God redeemed you through the precious blood of His dear Son, He placed, in the language of my illustration, a powerful engine under the hood—nothing less than the resurrection life of God the Son, made over to you in the person of God the Holy Spirit. Then stop pushing! Step in and switch on, and expose every hill of circumstance, of opportunity, of temptation, of perplexity—no matter how threatening—to the divine energy that is available.

With what magnificent confidence you may step out into the future when once you have consented to die to your own self-effort, and to make yourself available as a redeemed sinner to all that God has made available to you in His risen Son!"

Then he gives the real comparison of what it means to merely believe in or be in Christ, and what it would mean to let Christ or the Holy Spirit be in and work in you. He states:

"To be in *Christ*—that is redemption; but for Christ to be in *you*—that is sanctification! To be in *Christ*—that makes you fit for heaven; but for Christ to be in *you*—that makes you fit for earth! To be in *Christ*—that changes your destination; but for Christ to be in *you*—that changes your destiny! The one makes heaven your home—the other makes this world His workshop."

Indeed, to let Christ be in you can change your destination and destiny.

So much more can be done when we allow the Holy Spirit to work in us. As we often hear, God does not need our ability so much as He needs our availability. If we are available to Him and allow Him and the Holy Spirit to work in and through us, much can be accomplished to the glory of God, and for the benefit of all.

C. EXAMPLES OF A PERSONAL RELATIONSHIP

Early in this book I stated that I would mention a few experiences I had in a personal relationship with God and the Holy Spirit. I will mention a few, although there have been many recognizable to me for many years now. More than likely, He has been there all along, "trying" to guide me in the right direction and where I was "destined" to go. I was aware at times, and just too humanly stubborn to recognize or follow at other (perhaps most) times. He certainly can, and will, be with you, if you are willing to recognize Him. He is your conscience, for want of a better description.

In the Preface I mentioned about how I received aid from the Holy Spirit when writing a resolution for a bank I represented. I also indicated that my thought was, if I ever did that again I would tell it. Well, it did happen. I had been elected to the Court of Appeals, and about a year or two later, I was assigned to be the presiding judge on a difficult local government tax case. To say it came to us in a mess would be an understatement. The decision of the trial court was absolutely erroneous. The case had to be reversed, but neither side identified the problem, nor proposed a solution. I concluded that the case had to be reversed and remanded, but if that was all we do, it was going to come back again as bad as before. It was at that point I begin praying for some idea as to how this should be resolved. Perhaps some of my background helped, but I had never seen a situation like this one. Before long some clarity came to me like do this, and this, and then this, like ABC. I put those points in the opinion and directed that was what should be done. The other judges concurred, and the decision was rendered. It must have worked, as I do not believe we ever heard of that case again.

The point I want to make, however, is that roughly two weeks after the case had been rendered, I received a call from our chief staff attorney in the Frankfort office on another matter, but before we ended the conversation he said, "by the way, the way you ended that opinion was really neat." I said, "Well let me tell you about it." I told him exactly how it happened. There was a long pause. I think this shot right over his head, but finally he said, "Well, I guess the longer you are on the court the easier these things get." That may be true, but time in service had nothing to do with how that opinion was resolved. I had no regret for making that statement, because perhaps it may have planted a seed. Someday he may realize exactly what I was talking about. Something similar may happen to him, and then there can be an "A'ha moment."

Undoubtedly the longest sustained period of an ongoing personal relationship experience I have ever had occurred during the time when I was running for election to the court. This was in 1976. I had been nominated as one of three to be appointed for a position in division 2 of the 1st appellate district on the newly created Court of Appeals. What had been the Court of Appeals became the Supreme Court. There would be fourteen judges, two from each appellate district.

The governor had the right to make all original appointments. For division 1 of District 1, he had appointed my brother-n-law, who was eminently qualified, and was already a commissioner on the former

Court of Appeals. Naturally, the governor had to appoint one of the other nominees, and to make matters worse for him, I was a Republican in a heavy Democrat area. Whatever, had he appointed me, I would have had to give credit to him, but as it turned out, I was free to give credit where such was due. That would include all who helped me in any way with time, money, and ideas, and as you will see, God and The Holy Spirit. In hindsight, I truly believe that God had some plan for my life.

The campaign was one miracle after another. When the campaign was over, and the news media began asking how it happened, my response was that during the whole time, it was like someone was leading me around by the hand. Feelings of do this, go there, and don't do that occurred during the whole time. I had prayed for guidance before deciding to enter the race, and if it was His Will, then I was ready, but I would need help, including people and money. It all came, and it was substantial enough of a victory, that no one ever opposed me for this court until I retired twenty years later.

I will give you a couple of examples of the type of things that became common occurrences while campaigning. Time was a big factor, and it was short for covering twenty-three counties in Western Kentucky, but everything seemed to fall in place.

During a busy day in a distant county, among other things I hoped to find and visit with three people I knew and wanted to ask for help. I stopped at a radio station hoping to see the salesperson, who was also an active Republican in that county. Not only was she there at that time, but also the other two happened to come in. One was a banker, and the other a person active in local government. They had no idea I would be there, and, indeed, they had no reason to be looking for me. For that matter, I cannot imagine why the three would ever be in that place at the same time. I have no idea about the politics of the other two, but keep in mind that the new judgeships were to be nonpartisan. It was necessary to look for help wherever possible.

That leads me to another miracle. I attended a big Carter-Mondale Democrat rally in Hopkinsville. There must have been three thousand people there. Although I had some friends in Hopkinsville, I cannot remember seeing any on that occasion. I was on my own. I first stood outside and greeted the people as they arrived, then went inside and took a seat at a table. The master of ceremonies introduced all the candidates for all offices, but when he introduced the candidates for the Court of Appeals, he introduced the other party as "our candidate," and he introduced me as the "other candidate."

We can never be sure how people will react to such as that, but the people at my table had a fit. I happened to be sitting next to a man who was the area's outstanding and most loved radio personality. If he said something, it was believed. He asked me to come to his station for an interview, which I most certainly did. Perhaps he had to make a similar offer to the other candidate, but he gave me a good interview.

The president of a local bank was sitting across from me, and he invited me to visit him. I did, and he introduced me favorably to the employees and other people in the bank and in that vicinity.

Also, sitting at the table was a lady who happened to be the sister of someone I knew in Paducah. In the end, the lady, and her sister, had a party for me in Hopkinsville where I was able to find more support.

The mischief some intend can be reversed when God has other plans.

I will give you one more example of how a word of knowledge or a miracle can work. As always, time was of the essence. I had had a busy time in Muhlenberg and McLean Counties and stayed overnight with a friend, the next day, I worked in Butler County (with wonderful, yet surprising help), and then moved on to Simpson County for an open-house reception given by the mayor and attended by some of the most politically active people in that area. After that I had several things to do before finishing the day. I needed to take a newspaper ad, and a radio ad to Russellville, and also to give some campaign material to a man who was helping me, but who lived North of Russellville. I was also due in Bowling Green around four that afternoon to tape a TV interview. I was concerned about the drive to Bowling Green with all of the school buses which would be on the highway and slowing traffic.

Well, as it turned out, just as I pulled up to the newspaper office and was getting out of my car, I heard someone yell, "Hey, Bill." It was the man I was to give the campaign material to. He placed the newspaper ad for me, took the tape to the radio station, and took all the material I had brought along for him to dispense. I was not only able to leave early and have an easy drive to the TV station, but it also saved me from having to double back that evening to find him.

He had no idea I was going to be in Russellville at that time, nor did I have any thought of seeing him at that time. Whatever, the timing was perfect and I was certainly giving thanks and praise. This was more than a mere coincidence.

I could give more examples, but by now, you should get the picture.

The final point I will make concerning having a personal relationship with God, and knowing and doing His Will, can be illustrated with this situation. I often pray to know His Will, and to have the wherewithal to do it.

Sometime after receiving the Malcolm Smith tapes from Mrs. Boone, and studying them, and certainly after also studying the Rick Godwin tapes explaining the seven feasts of Israel, I began getting rather strong urges to start writing about all of it and sharing what I was learning with others.

Especially during the final several years I was on the court, the urging continued. I would get feelings, that I have been put in this position. My job especially involved writing opinions. I attended an appellate judge writing school. The "grooming" was ongoing. During the entire time I was on the court, I wrote roughly 2,600 opinions, of which over 285 were published. (Our criterion for what was published was based on what the decision added to the body of the law, and not the quality of the writing).

I retired in 1996 and got involved in other activities. As far as law was concerned, I began doing mediations and arbitrations to help people bring finality to their problems without spending a fortune on trial and appellate expenses. All the while I was looking after my cousin's affairs and establishing a Charitable Foundation. I finally had to quit all the legal activity and concentrate on my cousin's affairs and on the work of the foundation established by her.

Nevertheless, my mind never got far from the "call" to write. Yet, as I kept putting things off, I kept learning more and more, which just made it harder to put everything together without writing a whole library.

In July 2012, I got a real wake-up call, and I finally and seriously made up my mind that I really had to do this. One day I got a haircut, and after that I had an appointment for a massage, which was located at the barber shop. My children had given me gift certificates for the massages. I scheduled this one for an hour and a half, which I had not done before. An hour was usually the maximum, and thirty minutes might suffice for the neck and shoulders, or the feet. It turned out that I had to leave early to get ready to attend a luncheon. The luncheon was at a local hospital, and one of those who would be there was the mother of the masseuse.

She was not there, and when I had an opportunity to inquire, I learned that something had happened at her daughter's shop, so she had to leave. I called as soon as I could to find out what happened. Her father, an attorney in Paducah, answered, and explained. I went to see the damage as soon as I could.

Praise the Lord, no one was injured, but the shop was a mess, especially Elizabeth's area. It was totally destroyed, and a car had run over her desk and chair and was sitting on top of her massage table. When I left, and she had some free time, she went to the bank. A few minutes after she left, an elderly lady who was going to a beauty shop next door tried to park in front of the barber shop. She hit the accelerator rather than the brake, jumped the curb, and crashed right over everything in the way.

Of course, I was sorry for the lady, the barbers, and all the destruction, but what came to my mind was that still small voice which we hear when we really listen. The voice was not audible, but what it was telling me was: "I want you to pay attention. Your life will not go on forever, and for that matter, it can be snuffed out in a moment. Now get busy." One can say, I got my orders. I could just see myself, and Elizabeth, dead and crushed by or under that car. That did it, and I began to get serious about writing this book. It still did not come easy, and I had to get organized and reassemble much material, but what you see is what you get.

Before leaving this chapter, let me say that you, too, can have a personal relationship with Jesus Christ and the Holy Spirit. Let Christ be in you. Listen, pay attention to the "coincidences." They just may be God-created coincidences. Give thanks and praise and stay alert for the next one. Letting Christ be in you, can absolutely change your destiny, not just your destination.

D. THE REST OF THE STORY

"Many are the plans in a man's heart; but it is the Lord's purpose that prevails." Proverbs 19:21

That proverb is so true, as will be illustrated in "the rest of the story."

Without repeating many of the facts and details I have already written concerning a personal relationship, allow me to digress to the year 1990. In 1990, the Supreme Court justice from my appellate district retired. My term on the court of appeals did not end until 1991, therefore allowing me to run for the vacancy while keeping my position. "My plan" was to do that, and I did. To make a long story short, I lost. In legal parlance, one might say that my "Motion to advance to the Supreme Court" was "denied." Unbeknown to me at that time, God had His own plan which later prevailed.

During the campaign, there were no little miracles like those that occurred in 1976. The result was close, and the vote in one county near my home seemed to be reversed from what was expected. I asked for a review of that vote total but did not have any of my supporters view the tally sheets. When informed by an official that the numbers were correct, I conceded.

Naturally, I was disappointed, especially for all who had supported me, but I simply concluded that it was not part of God's Will for me. The winner was a friend, a rock-solid Christian, and one of the finest trial judges in Kentucky. The court would be in good hands.

In 1991, I ran for reelection to the Court of Appeals, and was unopposed. The eight-year term would last until 1999. Had I won the Supreme Court race, that term would have ended in 1998. I can say with almost 100% certainty that had I won, I would not have retired until the term ended.

However, I had no compelling reason to finish out the new term on the Court of Appeals. Miraculously, everything seemed to come together in October 1996. I had my sixty-fifth birthday, reached the maximum on my judicial retirement, became eligible for Social Security and Medicare all the same month. I also had the opportunity to begin taking care of my cousin's business, as well as do some mediating and arbitrating. In so many ways, I was much better off.

I still had to get my continuing legal education credits, so in May 1997, I attended a seminar in Boston on charitable-giving techniques. To make another long story short, a charitable foundation was born in September 1997. It originally had only a minimum amount in it and a remainder trust was created to pour into it after the death of my cousin and her husband. Funding of the remainder trust provided significant tax breaks, and the income she could receive was substantially more than the dividend income provided by the stock sold to create the trust. In 2003, the foundation was significantly funded, and we began making grants.

After providing for a daughter and three grandchildren, my cousin and her husband decided to leave the bulk of their estates to the foundation upon their deaths.

Anyone could and would tell you that the foundation has provided generously for Christian ministries, education, and missions; locally, and the world over. It has also benefited local hospitals and cultural activities and supported entities defending our Judeo-Christian heritage in this country.

God's plan prevailed, but I can only wonder how all of this might have played out, had my plan prevailed. Indeed, God had a much better plan for me too. I could not see it in 1990, but in retrospect, it is clear. If your plan does not prevail, do not despair. God may have a better plan for you, although unknown at that time. Be open to it, look for it, and accept it.

This incident also illustrates the meaning of Romans 8:28, which reads:

"And we know that in all things God works for the good of those who love him, who have been called according to his purpose."

Although I have been able to see God's hand in my life, and have benefited from good things, I have had to be disciplined and suffer consequences for bad decisions and disobeying God's laws and commandments. On occasion, "my Shepherd" has extended His crook out to stop me and pull me back in line, or at least get my attention.

Open your heart, eyes, and mind and see Jesus's involvement in your life.

✝

CHAPTER 7

WHAT CHRISTIANS BELIEVE

"Believe in the Lord Jesus, and you will be saved."
ACTS 16:31

That scripture sounds simple enough, but it is only the beginning for what brings salvation. There is much more to it, and not all who merely say they believe will be saved. Christians believe that they not only must believe in Jesus Christ but also are to be baptized; repent of their sins, that is to be truthfully sorry for the sinful things each of us has done; and to convert, that is change our ways and future habits, so that, thereafter, we can better obey God's laws and commands.

The Bible makes it quite clear that while we are all invited to His table, not all will make it. See Luke 14: 24. Even those who have been enlightened may "fall away." See Hebrews 6: 4-7. Many will refuse to participate or to even believe. Many refuse to recognize they are sinful and feel they are in no need of a savior, and especially those who refuse to believe there is anything more than this life on Earth. I think of the parable of the Pharisee and the tax collector in Luke 18:9-14. The

Pharisee exalted himself, apparently refused to believe he was a sinner, while the tax collector was so ashamed that he refused to even look up. Jesus concluded that the tax collector was the one justified, and then added: "For everyone who exalts himself will be humbled, and he who humbles himself will be exalted."

Some believe that "once saved, always saved." While I would like to believe in that concept, I have my doubts. I believe the Bible is clear in its totality, that man can fall away, resign his faith and belief, deny Jesus and lose his salvation and his seat at the "banquet." Much of our remaining in God's grace, is what is in our heart; and perhaps, in that sense, the individual never sincerely believed and was not saved in the first place. Maybe he joined for social reasons or show, never grew in his faith, or truly repented and converted. Only God knows our heart and true feelings. That type of judging is out of my league. I was never trained in Ecclesiastical law. Maybe the theory of "once saved, always saved" became popular as a way to make it easier for people to come to a belief in Jesus in the first place, such as the idea of a pretribulation rapture, which is discussed in chapter 8. Certainly, once the "seed" was planted and with a "sinner" in a loving Church family, there was an opportunity for growth and the development of his soul. However, Jesus made it clear that the way was "narrow," we would be persecuted for believing in Him, and that we must take up our "cross" and follow Him. Christians must be taught and understand these things in order not to "fall away" in difficult times and situations.

Let us not forget that we are saved by faith in Jesus Christ and only through the Grace of God. (Period.) We cannot earn it by our good works, lest we might boast, but likewise faith without some works on behalf of the Kingdom of God is "dead faith." See Ephesians 2:8, and James 2:26, but generally, 2:14-26.

While there may seem to be apparent conflict between what Paul taught, that is, we are saved by grace through faith and not by works; and what James wrote, in that faith without works is dead faith. Let us make no mistake, our salvation comes by the GRACE of God (i.e., unmerited, undeserved favor) through FAITH and belief in Jesus Christ. However, if there is true belief and faith and love in and for Jesus Christ there will be works and obedience to his laws and commands. Our salvation cannot be earned by works. Salvation was purchased by the sacrifice of Jesus' body and blood in creating the New Covenant. To secure and confirm passage for your soul on the "Heavenly Express," your requirement is to believe in Jesus and what he did, repent of your sins, seek His forgiveness, and trust and obey Him and His commandments.

Christians believe in the Ten Commandments, but also the summary of the law as given by Jesus, which was to love God with your whole heart, soul, and mind, and to love your neighbor as yourself. God and Jesus are love and they taught us to love one another, and to forgive one another.

Christians believe in heaven and in hell. They believe that the Bible in totality gives history, (which could be stated "His Story") beginning with creation and the fall of man from paradise, followed by the efforts of God to reconnect with mankind and bring us back to a relationship and eternal life with Him in paradise or heaven.

Jesus made it quite clear that no one comes to the Father in heaven except through Him. In John 14:6 we read: Jesus answered, "I am the way and the truth and the life. No one comes to the Father except through me." Make no mistake. If you do not accept Jesus as your Lord and Savior, and believe in the sacrifice He made for you, you are destined to spend eternity elsewhere.

Jesus requires that we profess our faith and belief in Him publicly. Generally, this would happen when one joins a church or a body of believers. Jesus told His followers: "Whoever acknowledges me before others, I will also acknowledge before my Father in heaven. [33]But whoever disowns me before others, I will disown before my Father in heaven." (Matthew 10:32-33) It seems clear that if we acknowledge Jesus publicly, He will know us, but if we deny Him, He will not know us.

He has also given us commands to follow and action to take. The "great commission" applies to all believers. It is found in Matthew 28:19-20, and it provides: "[19]Therefore go and make disciples of all nations, baptizing them in the name of the Father and of the Son and of the Holy Spirit, [20]and teaching them to obey everything I have commanded you. And surely, I am with you always, to the very end of the age." It appears that we are expected to do more than merely believe.

The title to this chapter may seem a bit redundant. After all, all I have previously written has been to help everyone *understand* what Christianity is all about. This was done to help explain Christianity to nonbelievers, but also to help Christians solidify and strengthen their faith and guide them in the *development of their souls*. The objective was also to enable anyone to answer questions for themselves, and to help others become believers in Jesus Christ. I do hope you now understand who Jesus was, what He did, and why and how He did what He did, and that He did it for YOU.

It is also clear that *everything is His*, and that with the covenant He made with God the Father on our behalf, we are coheirs with Him and will share in the inheritance and in living with Him eternally. This is how we are the undeserving third-party beneficiaries of Jesus's covenant with God the Father.

It is perhaps a good thing to summarize what we have been learning and what Christians need to know and believe. Now, my challenge to you comes from 2 Timothy 2:2, "And the things you have heard me say in the presence of many witnesses entrust to reliable people who will also be qualified to teach others." Do it. Carry out the "great commission." Join the winning team. Get to know the leader and allow Him to know you. "The harvest is plentiful, but the workers are few. [38]Ask the Lord of the harvest, therefore, to send out workers into his harvest field." (Matthew 9:37-38)

The Christian Church does have a creed. As a matter of fact, there are two generally accepted creeds. "The Apostle's Creed" and the creed which is commonly called "The Nicene Creed," adopted in AD 325. The latter is longer and more detailed, but the Apostle's Creed covers the essentials, and is perhaps more widely used. The Modern English Version reads:

> "*I believe in God the Father* almighty, Creator of heaven and earth.
>
> *I believe in Jesus Christ, God's only Son, our Lord*, who was conceived by the Holy Spirit, born of the Virgin Mary, suffered under Pontius Pilate, *was crucified, died, and was buried*, he descended to the dead. On the third day *he rose again*, he ascended into heaven, he is seated at the right hand of the Father, and he will come again to judge the living and the dead.
>
> *I believe in the Holy Spirit*, the holy catholic church, the communion of Saints, *the forgiveness of sins, the resurrection of the body, and the life everlasting*. Amen." (Emphasis added)

Not all churches recite the Creed in their regular services, but many denominations do. Nevertheless, all baptized believers believe in the essence of The Apostle's Creed. It gives us the concept of the trinity with Father, Son, and Holy Spirit. It also tells that Jesus was the Son of God, He was conceived by the Holy Spirit, and born of a virgin by the name of Mary. We also know that He was sentenced to death and suffered terribly under Pontius Pilate. He was crucified and He died and was buried. He went to the place of the dead, but on the third day He arose from the dead. Following His resurrection, He ascended into heaven where He sits with His Father, God Almighty, and in the future, He will come to judge the living and the dead.

The Creed continues by saying that we believe in the holy catholic church, the communion of saints, the forgiveness of sins, the resurrection of the body, and in Eternal Life. If the term "catholic" should give you a problem, just consider the word means "universal." It does not mean Roman, Orthodox, Anglican, or any specific denomination. It is the universal Church of Jesus Christ.

Christians believe that the Bible is true and is the Word of God from God. Christians believe that all men and women are sinners and that we fall short in how we should live. Keep in mind that merely thinking of violating any of God's commandments is itself a sin. Let us not argue about the point. We are all sinners in the eyes of God. (Period) Nevertheless, we are forgiven by God's grace, when we repent and are truly sorry and ask for forgiveness. Remember, however, that to be forgiven, we must forgive those that offend or harm us.

While God is love and is loving, He has rules which must be obeyed. The commandments make it clear that sexual relations outside of marriage are sins. The Bible teaches that "marriage" is between a man and a woman, political correctness and the U.S. Supreme Court to the contrary notwithstanding. Biblically speaking, from the time of Adam and Eve, the man and the woman were to be fruitful and multiply and to create a family.

One of the other commandments which is significant for me is the one that prohibits the giving of false testimony or false swearing. Indeed, our courts of law could be made a mockery of if all testimony was given without the fear of some damnation for lying under oath. Truth is an essential element in life. Although there are laws and penalties against perjury, in these days I cannot help but wonder just how effective an oath to tell the truth might be.

Christians worship corporately, together with other believers. Although many may think it is wonderful to observe God's beautiful creation while on the golf course, this is not a real way to worship and learn the word of God or to become strong in your faith and develop your soul. If you do not already belong to a group of believers, I certainly urge you to do that. However, I would also urge you to be careful as to what group you associate with. Political correctness has so corrupted our society, our government, and many churches that some denominations can now be considered denominations of accommodation standing for nothing. Unfortunately, in the United ApoStates of America, if something is thought to be biblically correct, it must be expunged and wiped clean from our society and even our thoughts. The atheists and humanists have effectively done the devil's work.

Some churches may be in a beautiful building, but don't become subject to an edifice complex. As sinners we are all in need of a solid Bible believing and teaching church. The church, and body of Christ, where you worship, must prepare and equip you for what you need now and for what is yet to come.

There are many differences in corporate worship and the denominations that have been formed. Few differences really have anything to do with your ultimate salvation. All churches should observe at least two sacraments. They would be Baptism and Holy Communion, or as it is otherwise called, the Lord's Supper or the Eucharist. Sacraments are the things ordained by Jesus Christ. He ordained Baptism and He ordained the Lord's Supper or Communion. Each of the Christ-ordained sacraments has a visible and outward sign for an inward and spiritual grace. Some churches, however, do have other ceremonies which they identify as sacraments. They would include confirmation, penance, orders, matrimony, and extreme unction.

As to the two universal sacraments, they, too, are observed in different manners. Some denominations baptize infants shortly after their birth and have sponsors (Godparents) to help raise them properly until the time they can publicly profess their faith and be confirmed. Such baptisms are usually by sprinkling blessed Holy water. Other denominations do not baptize until the believer has publicly acknowledged his belief and faith in Jesus Christ. Some of those may baptize by sprinkling, but others baptize by immersion.

I would be the last to say that either method is absolutely correct or incorrect. Both follow long-standing traditions. Either method would meet the definition of a sacrament in that it is an outward sign of an inward and spiritual grace. What is correct for the individual should be based on the feeling they have in their heart.

However, it just seems to me to be more appropriate for immersion in that it is symbolic of the death, burial, and resurrection of Jesus Christ as well as being done in the name of God the Father, Jesus Christ the Son, and the Holy Spirit.

The Jewish baptism was more of a cleansing ritual or washing away of sin. It could have been performed by the sprinkling of water, or by immersion, but when John the Baptist was standing in the river Jordan, it is difficult for me to visualize that he was merely sprinkling water. I also find it significant that the Apostle Paul wrote in Romans 6:3-5:

> [3]Or don't you know that all of us who were baptized into Christ Jesus were baptized into his death? [4]We were therefore buried with him through baptism into death in order that, just as Christ was raised from the dead through the glory of the Father, we too may live a new life.
>
> [5]For if we have been united with him in a death like his, we will certainly also be united with him in a resurrection like his.

I was originally baptized by immersion, but my wife and six children were baptized as infants by sprinkling. However, four of the six children have since been baptized by immersion, and in 1997, my wife was baptized by immersion in the Jordan River.

The celebration of the sacrament of the Lord's Supper, Holy Communion, or Eucharist is performed in different ways. The participants also believe differently about the significance of what they receive. Some believe that in the ceremony of the Mass, the bread and wine become the body and blood of Jesus Christ. Others believe that it is merely symbolic of the flesh and blood of Jesus Christ. It is always done as a required remembrance of Jesus and the sacrifice He made for us by creating the "new blood covenant." Personally, I know what I am receiving but I can feel I am somehow spiritually receiving the body and blood of the Christ. He told us what it represented and to do it in remembrance of Him every time we received it. I can certainly do that.

Another point I will make is that Christians believe that all things come from God. He owns the universe, and whatever we have comes from Him. We owe Him our tithes, which include our time, our talent, and our money. As Christians we give back to support Him, the Church, and the spread of the Gospel (the Good News) worldwide. We give to our church and to Christian ministries and missions.

Finally, Christians pray. We pray for ourselves, others, our communities and leaders, and for God's Kingdom. We give praise and thanks, and we pray for forgiveness, and for a forgiving spirit. We do not need anyone to pray on our behalf, as we now have direct access to the Father through our belief in Jesus Christ. The veil before the Holy of Holies in the Temple was torn from top to bottom when Jesus was crucified. Christians need to develop a habit and discipline of praying. There is no limit on the types or purposes of prayers, but I will close this chapter with one final thought.

If you have not yet given your heart to Jesus and become a Christian, but you now wish to do so, then sincerely pray this prayer, or something like it. You can certainly pray whatever is in your heart. Also, for those who are professed Christians, but who have moved to the inactive list, you might also want to give thanks and praise as you come back into the fold. What follows is meant as an example, so use it as you see fit.

Father in Heaven, I give you all thanks and praise. Thanks for all you have done for me, and for opening my eyes to the knowledge and understanding of Jesus Christ, and the sacrifice He made for me by giving His blood and dying on that horrible cross. Thank you, Jesus. I praise you, Father, for who and what you are. I thank you for my life and the lives of my loved ones.

Father, I acknowledge that I am a sinner, and that I am truly sorry for all of my sins and transgressions against you and your Holiness, and against my fellow man. I humbly pray for your forgiveness, and I pray that with the Holy Spirit I will hereafter live as you would have me to live and follow your commandments. I pray, too, that I will be always alert to the Holy Spirit and feel His conviction anytime I sin by thought, word, or deed. I give thanks to the Holy Spirit for the Gift of Faith received by me.

Father, I believe that your Son Jesus died to atone for my sins, and the sins of the world, and that you raised Him from death to be the first for all of us in the final harvest of all souls, including me, for which I am eternally thankful.

I confess that Jesus Christ is Lord in my heart and soul, and I believe in Him and accept Him right now as my Lord and Savior. Give me a contrite heart as I repent for my sins. Guard and guide me, and show me Your Will for me, as I go forth to live by following the path you set before me. May I bring honor and glory to you and not me.

Father, thank you for your forgiving grace, and for adopting me and making me an heir to your eternal kingdom. I praise you, love you, and thank you from all of my heart.

In the name of Jesus, the Christ, I pray, Amen.

Now, if you are a new Christian, I urge you to continue with these suggestions. Tell someone about your new faith. Be baptized as soon as you can. Get a Bible and begin studying it and get with a group of believers for your study. Share your faith with them. You might read some of the books I refer to in the appendix. Most will be very helpful, at least for specific purposes. Find a good Bible-believing-and-teaching Church where you will be comfortable with the fellowship to be found there. My wife and I are now Baptist, but I am a firm believer that when that final role is called, the Heavenly realm will be filled with Christians from many and various denominations, which are all part of The Church of Jesus Christ.

We are commanded to love God, and if you truly believe what you have been learning, and understand what He has done for you, and will do, then certainly you do love Him. If you love someone, you will want to spend time with that person, and learn more and improve your relationship. Prayer and some quiet time are a good way to be in God's presence. Make it a habit, and ask God to help you increase your faith, and to have a better and fuller understanding of His Word (the Bible).

God's grace will be sufficient for all your real needs, but it is not a cheap grace. Give Him your best. He is worthy and let us never forget what Jesus has done for each of us. Keep the covenant relationship, and continuously develop your soul. What could be worth more?

Christians must recognize Jesus not only as Savior, but Lord. You will be glad to let the town drunk save you, if you are drowning in the river, but for one who is Lord, He is your master and the one to be followed and obeyed. One of my all-time favorite hymns is "Trust and Obey," written by John H. Sammis. The meaningful words to me are: "When we walk with the Lord, in the light of His word, what a glory He sheds on our way; while we do His good will, He abides with us still, and to all who will trust and obey. Trust and obey, for there's no other way to be happy in Jesus, than to trust and obey."

Stay with Him. Get to know Him. Obey Him. You cannot lose. Get active. Do something to help Him and the Kingdom of God. Do not be a weed or one of the tares. Such will be going nowhere, and remember, to bear fruit and win others, you are nothing without Him. John 15:4-5 makes that point very clear. Jesus was speaking to His disciples, and said,

[4]Remain in me, as I also remain in you. No branch can bear fruit by itself; it must remain in the vine. Neither can you bear fruit unless you remain in me.

⁵"I am the vine; you are the branches. If you remain in me and I in you, you will bear much fruit; apart from me you can do nothing.

To all, I close with this challenge. Grow in your faith, trust, and understanding. Become rock solid and be prepared for anything. When times get tough, many of the weak and uncertain in their belief will fall away. Do not become one of those.

As you live your life, keep developing your soul. "Let your light shine before others, that they may see your good deeds and glorify your Father in heaven." Matthew 5:16.

Let me also challenge you to raise your Christian "religion" to a personal relationship with God, Jesus and the Holy Spirit. Many of you will have had such experiences, but others will not. A way to begin could be alone or with a study group by asking yourself, what has been my closest moment with God this day or this week? It could be an answer to a prayer, or an unusual occurrence, which had to be due to some outside interference. Some might dismiss the event as a mere coincidence, but at least consider that it might be a God created coincidence. Recognition of a Godly encounter can be a joyful and blessed experience.

If the occurrence would lead to Godly results and good things in keeping with His commandments and laws, you can know from whence it came. However, be discerning, as "Satan can masquerade as an Angel of Light" and loves to cause trouble. II Corinthians 11:14. We learn in I Peter 5:8 ". . . be self-controlled and alert. Your enemy the devil prowls around like a roaring lion looking for someone to devour." If the encounter would lead to violations of God's laws and commandments, then recognize the source and avoid the situation.

✝

CHAPTER 8

THE FUTURE—
LOOKING AHEAD

"¹⁶Three times a year all your men must appear before the Lord
your God at the place he will choose: at the Festival of Unleavened
Bread, the Festival of Weeks and the Festival of Tabernacles."
DEUTERONOMY 16:16

A. THE FEAST OF TABERNACLES

We have studied about the seven feasts and should know and understand that in the first month of the Jewish religious calendar they were to celebrate Passover, Unleavened Bread, and First Fruits. Israel experienced Passover and Unleavened Bread when they first made the Exodus from Egypt. Experientially they also had it when Jesus, the perfect Lamb of God, went to the cross and shed his blood. We received salvation through the blood of Christ which removes all sin. Unleavened Bread speaks to us of putting sin out. If you have any form of leaven in you, your house, your work, or your church, put it out. We celebrate Passover and Unleavened Bread in the Church today, when we receive

Holy Communion, or the Lord's Supper. This is the "covenant meal" Christians are to observe as prescribed by Jesus for the New Covenant.

First Fruits was required when the Israelites moved into the Promised Land and they were to present a sheaf of the first growth as a wave offering. It speaks to us today as the resurrection of Jesus, and we celebrate it in the Church today in baptism representing Jesus's death, burial, and resurrection.

The Feast of Pentecost or Weeks was a third-month feast. It was an early harvest and not the full harvest. It was incomplete and was merely on the way to something bigger and better. God visited His people roughly fifty days after they left Egypt when they were in the desert at Mount Sinai. The Israelites were commanded to keep this feast when they entered the Promised Land. The Holy Spirit came to the Jews in Jerusalem fifty days after the resurrection of Jesus. The Spirit came with power and enabled the disciples to begin the new church. The disciples were empowered by the Spirit, and on that first day they brought in a harvest of new believers numbering at least three thousand men.

We can also see a parallel picture with the tabernacle of Moses or the Temple. We have the outer court and the first-month feasts of Passover where we get Jesus and have the beginning. This would also symbolize the thirty-fold Christians. In the inner court we have Pentecost where we receive the gifts of the Spirit and power. For those that are willing to move into the inner court, they could do more and be the sixty-fold producers. Finally in the Holy of Holies would be the Feast of Tabernacles with the full harvest. Those willing to move on to Tabernacles would have the fullness of God and become hundred-fold producing Christians.

Many of the Israelites did not want to leave Egypt. Many were reluctant to leave Sinai. Still more were reluctant to go into the Promised Land when they had the opportunity, and along the way many died, or were left behind. Even at Sinai when God spoke, many of the people told Moses do not let Him speak to us again, you go talk to Him. So today we have Christians still staying at Passover without the fullness that God offers through sanctification with the Holy Spirit. Don't stop where you are. Keep going. There is more. God told the Israelites that they had been camped at Sinai long enough and to go and possess the land. Not all did, and not all will move on now.

There was a quiet time following Pentecost. For the next three months the crops merely grew. They were aided by the latter rain, and in the seventh month they were ready for the ingathering of the wine, the oil, the corn, the fruit, and the full harvest. The Israelites were told to commemorate this with a Feast of Trumpets on the first day of the seventh month. On the tenth day of that month, they would have the Day of Atonement. Beginning on the fifteenth of the seventh month, and continuing for seven days, they would celebrate the Feast of Tabernacles. These were described in more detail previously.

The Feast of Trumpets speaks of preparation. It is to awaken and alarm the people and to tell them to get ready. They are to put off sin and prepare for their atonement. The congregation was to assemble. The Day of Atonement was a one-day, twenty-four-hour time for perfection and cleansing. It was a time for repentance. In ancient Israel this was the one day a year that the high priest would go beyond the veil of the Temple and into the Holy of Holies to petition God for the people. This was the day for the cleansing of the nation and all the people.

I sometimes believe I already hear those trumpets blowing. Indeed, with all of the signs showing up these days, it is time to be alert, to be watchful, and to be prepared for whatever.

When the fulfillment of the Day of Atonement comes that will be the time when Jesus cleanses His Church. Whatever that cleansing involves, everyone will go through it. It may be what is called the tribulation. It will be a time when the wheat is separated from the tares or weeds. Israel never bypassed the problems, although God protected them from the plagues in Egypt. Likewise, Noah did not bypass the flood, but stayed through it.

For perhaps as long as the past two hundred years, many preachers teach an easy, comfortable, and cheap grace. If you believe, and get on board the Gospel train, and if things get bad, God will take you out. Such teaching, known as a pretribulation rapture, has allowed for much laxity to grow in the Church(s). I have no definite idea of where or how or from whom such theology began, but whatever or however, I personally question the doctrine for reasons I will present later in the section on the Rapture.

When Jesus returns, He will be coming for a pure bride (His Church). It will be a time for cleansing and separation, and not all will be received in, just as only five of the ten virgins were received when the bridegroom came. Also consider the story of the servant who was given a talent (money in those days) but did nothing with it. It was taken away and given to another, and the sluggard was thrown out into eternal darkness. Both stories are found in Matthew, Chapter 25. The stories follow immediately after Jesus explained to His disciples the signs of the end times, the end of the age, or of His return.

Here is a final thought on the idea that believers will not have to be tested and will avoid any "tribulation." If that is the case, how can anyone explain what is happening today in the Middle East with the persecution of Christians and Jews? If that would not be classified as tribulation, I have no definition for it. We can see, however, that these Christians are standing firm and passing the test. When Jesus separates the wheat from tares, these martyrs will have passed the ultimate test, and their destination to paradise will be sealed. How strong is your faith and belief?

The first four feasts have been fulfilled, but Tabernacles is yet to come. The Church has not yet experienced Tabernacles, but it will when Jesus comes back for his spotless and clean bride (The Church). The Church appears to be far from that pure and spotless condition at this time, but it could be cleansed quickly. Tabernacles will be accompanied with power and universality. It will be a festival of unity and joy, and a display of God's glory. It will be a festival of restoration wherein everything is made whole and right. It will bring a new thing, and many new souls will be added and saved. People of all beliefs will be converting very quickly, and unlike anything ever seen before.

B. WHEN WILL THESE THINGS HAPPEN?

My short answer is that I do not know, nor do I believe that anyone knows. Jesus made it clear that no one knows, except the Father. What and when He chooses to do something will be in His own perfect time. However, what we can do is to look at the prophesies and observe the signs that are appearing. With all of the prophesies already fulfilled, I have no reason to believe that Tabernacles and the return of Jesus will not happen. When we have a close look, it does appear that the time may be getting closer when Jesus will return, and the world will be ruled by Him.

One of the more compelling signs is that the prophecy that the Jews would return to the Promised Land is being fulfilled. Not long ago, no one would have thought this could ever happen. This miracle is on par with the Exodus and the Resurrection.

A big error made by Christian theologians was that the Jews were no longer under covenant with God. The Temple was destroyed in AD 70, and the Jews were scattered (diaspora) all over the world. They were persecuted and forced out of one place after another. A new doctrine emerged holding that Israel had been replaced by The Christian Church. This was known as "replacement theology." This thinking led to or allowed for everything from the expulsion of Jews from many places down to Hitler's furnaces. It is the source of Jewish hatred and serious anti-Semitism. Where The Church should have defended and helped the Jews, it failed.

Allow me to digress, or take a brief detour, for consideration of a few questions. Who is going to lose when Jesus returns? Who is raging against the fulfillment of Jesus's return? Who stands to gain by destroying all of the Jews? (And Christians)? Who, or what groups, today are so vitriolic in hatred of the Jews? Who is stirring up much of the anti-Semitism? (And why)? Who, or on whose behalf, is promoting the complete annihilation of Israel, the Jews, and Judaism? You can fill in the blanks, and when you realize the answers, determine not to be a part of it. You are going to end up on the wrong side, the losing side. Get out of any such association. Malice and envy were on the list of "leavens," but for clarity, let's add "hatred." Put it out. Remember, to be forgiven, we must be forgiving. Learn to live by that rule.

Another question for me is why would or should anyone hate the Jews? The Temple hierarchy wanted Him out of the way and got Rome to do the job. However, His death was intended long before it happened. The Jews have done nothing to me, nor probably you either. Collectively, they have given this old world much in science, medicine, culture, and many good things. We all live better because of them. There is no telling what or how much civilization lost when those horrible furnaces were fired up.

What we are witnessing then and now is Kingdoms in Conflict 101. The Church must stop turning a blind eye to the situation, and more forcefully expose the situation and the instigators. It must bring those blindly participating in such activity and thoughts into a belief in Jesus Christ. Political correctness, to the contrary, must be "corrected."

Remember, if today's political environment could have its way, Christianity would be removed from public thought. The atheists and humanists are doing all they can to wipe religion, and especially Christianity, out of our lives. Indeed, the Church should and could get more involved in this situation, but historically and traditionally, we can see it has not.

The Church has been controlled by men, and not always by the holiest or most brilliant minds. Some of the historical leaders were filled and led by the Holy Spirit; but, as for many of the leaders, between politics, vain glory, and their personal quest for power and money, serious, tragic decisions were made. Among such would be efforts to challenge science and forcefully continue the theory that the earth is flat, the imprisonment of people such as Galileo, indulgences, anti-Semitism, and the inquisitions, are in this category. The crusades are often criticized but were of brief duration against centuries of Islamic jihad activity wherein millions of Christians and Jews were killed, persecuted, and enslaved. Hopefully, The Church will get purified soon in preparation for Jesus's return.

Whatever, a "restoration theology" is moving forward, and people are beginning to know that the Jews are still God's chosen people. Jesus was Jewish, and someday the Jewish holdouts will realize that He is the Messiah, Yeshua, and finally believe in Him. Many Jews already believe, and more are beginning to believe all the time.

Back to a consideration of the Jews' return to their homeland, certain rights were granted in the late nineteenth Century, and more around 1917, but little was done about it. Horrific efforts were made to make sure that their return would never happen, and, therefore, the prophetic return and reign of Jesus would never happen. Adolf Hitler's effort sought to have a "final solution" with the extermination of Jews. As horrible as that was, it was not completed, and the Holocaust was one of the sympathetic reasons the Jewish state of Israel was established in 1948.

The Jews did begin returning to their little sliver of land but were immediately fought by their Arab neighbors with the idea of driving them into the sea. Today, Iran threatens to destroy Israel and kill all of the Jews with atomic weapons now that Jews are bunched together in such a small space.

However, if you think the Jews are no longer in covenant with God, then it is time to rethink your position. Consider how they were able to defend themselves against such overwhelming odds. Consider also the many supernatural miracles that happened on their behalf to save them and to defeat their enemies. A thirteen-part cable TV documentary entitled *Against All Odds, Israel Survives* covers many of these miracles including the Yom Kippur War, the 1967 War, and the raid on the airport at Entebbe. This has been and may still be available on DVD.

Indeed, in 1967 while resisting another attempt to destroy them, the Israelis retook Jerusalem and established that as their capital. If there is a time clock attached to any of these events for the return of Jesus, it would seem to apply to the retaking of Jerusalem. However, the time could also begin in 1948 or 1949, when the "fig tree" (a symbol for Israel) was planted and survived an attempted uprooting by the Arab neighbors. It began putting out its leaves. See Matthew 24:32, another end of the age reference by Jesus.

Efforts continue to remove the Jews from Jerusalem, or at least to divide Jerusalem. But there are signs that this is not to be, and woe be unto those that do persecute Israel and attempt to divide the country or Jerusalem. It seems that when new efforts are made to divide Israel and create a Palestinian state, or to divide Jerusalem, natural calamities happen. Coincidence? Maybe, but maybe not. I have no doubt that God is in control. These events could be warnings.

Turning to the signs of the times, in Matthew 24, Mark 13, and Luke 21, Jesus tells his disciples what signs to look for at the end of the age. These passages are sometimes referred to as the "Olivet Discourse." In Matthew 24, Jesus was talking with his disciples at the temple and they brought his attention to the buildings. It was then that Jesus told them that the day was coming when not one stone would be left on another. Everyone would be thrown down. (The temple was destroyed in AD 70.) They moved on to the Mount of Olives and the disciples asked Jesus to tell them what would be the sign of your coming at the end of the age? These are two separate events. The destruction of the

Temple has happened, the "end of the age" or the return of Jesus has not. Beginning in Matthew 24:4-41 we read,

> ⁴Jesus answered: "Watch out that no one deceives you. ⁵For *many will come in my name*, claiming, 'I am the Messiah,' and will deceive many. ⁶You will hear of wars and rumors of wars, but see to it that you are not alarmed. Such things must happen, but the end is still to come. ⁷Nation will rise against nation, and kingdom against kingdom. *There will be famines and earthquakes in various places.* ⁸All these are the beginning of birth pains.
>
> ⁹"Then you will be handed over to *be persecuted and put to death*, and you will be *hated by all nations because of me.* ¹⁰At that time *many will turn away from the faith* and will betray and hate each other, ¹¹and *many false prophets will appear and deceive many people.* ¹²Because of the *increase of wickedness*, the love of most will grow cold, ¹³but *the one who stands firm to the end will be saved.* ¹⁴And *this gospel of the kingdom will be preached* in the whole world as a testimony *to all nations, and then the end will come.*
>
> ¹⁵"So *when you see standing in the holy place 'the abomination that causes desolation,' spoken of through the prophet Daniel*—let the reader understand—¹⁶then let those who are in Judea flee to the mountains. ¹⁷Let no one on the housetop go down to take anything out of the house. ¹⁸Let no one in the field go back to get their cloak. ¹⁹How dreadful it will be in those days for pregnant women and nursing mothers! ²⁰Pray that your flight will not take place in winter or on the Sabbath. ²¹For *then there will be great distress, unequaled from the beginning of the world until now—and never to be equaled again.*
>
> ²²"If those days had not been cut short, no one would survive, but *for the sake of the elect those days will be shortened.* ²³At that

time if anyone says to you, 'Look, here is the Messiah!' or, 'There he is!' do not believe it. ²⁴*For false messiahs and false prophets will appear and perform great signs and wonders to deceive, if possible, even the elect.* ²⁵See, I have told you ahead of time.

²⁶"So if anyone tells you, 'There he is, out in the wilderness,' do not go out; or, 'Here he is, in the inner rooms,' do not believe it. ²⁷*For as lightning that comes from the east is visible even in the west, so will be the coming of the Son of Man.* ²⁸Wherever there is a carcass, there the vultures will gather.

²⁹"*Immediately after the distress of those days the sun will be darkened, and the moon will not give its light; the stars will fall from the sky, and the heavenly bodies will be shaken.'*

³⁰"*Then will appear the sign of the Son of Man in heaven. And then all the peoples of the earth will mourn when they see the Son of Man coming on the clouds of heaven, with power and great glory.* ³¹*And he will send his angels with a loud trumpet call, and they will gather his elect from the four winds, from one end of the heavens to the other.*

³²"*Now learn this lesson from the fig tree: As soon as its twigs get tender and its leaves come out, you know that summer is near.* ³³Even so, *when you see all these things, you know that it is near,* right at the door. ³⁴Truly I tell you, this generation will certainly not pass away until all these things have happened. ³⁵Heaven and earth will pass away, but my words will never pass away.

³⁶"*But about that day or hour no one knows, not even the angels in heaven, nor the Son, but only the Father.* ³⁷*As it was in the days of Noah, so it will be at the coming of the Son of Man.* ³⁸For in the days before the flood, people were eating and drinking, marrying and giving in marriage, up to the day Noah entered the ark; ³⁹and *they knew nothing about what would happen until the flood came and took them all away. That is how it will be at the*

coming of the Son of Man. ⁴⁰ *Two men will be in the field; one will be taken and the other left.* ⁴¹ *Two women will be grinding with a hand mill; one will be taken and the other left.* (Emphasis added).

There is much to be gleamed from this explanation, but it must be broken down to be understood.

Jesus says there will be many pretending to be Him. I am not aware of any serious pretenders at this time, but such could begin at any time. He reiterates this in verses 23 and 24 saying that the false prophets and messiahs will deceive by performing "great signs and wonders." (Aided by Satan no less.)

He tells of famines and earthquakes. While we have had both historically, they appear to be increasing in numbers and severity. Droughts are ruining much of the best agricultural lands, and the number of earthquakes has vastly increased. While discussing the multiple numbers of earthquakes in the Oklahoma area, someone suggested it could be from "fracking." My wife responded that Jesus did not say why they would increase, but just that they would. (Good thinking.) The threat of more severe earthquakes is ever present.

Jesus said that His disciples and followers would be persecuted and hated. Indeed, it happened to His disciples, and today we can see the increasing persecution and hatred of His followers. It is getting worse, and it is not merely confined to the Middle East. Jesus said that there would be much distress, unequaled from the beginning of the world. As bad as situations have been in the past, I am not aware of more pure evil and wickedness than what we are now witnessing from ISIS and other radical Islamic jihadists. We can expect it to get worse, and worldwide. That is definitely possible.

The idea that those who stand firm to the end will be saved seems to contradict the concept of any pretribulation rapture. See Matthew 24:13.

Jesus says the Gospel (The Good News) will be preached and made available to everyone. Without some divine help this has not been possible until the most recent times. With the efforts of translators and many groups, together with modern technologies, the possibility of man's success in delivering the Word to the world has never been greater. However, to any extent that man fails, God will get it done as Heaven sees fit.

Jesus tells us not to believe the "false sightings." When He returns, just as lightning can be seen from East to West, He will be seen by all. You ask, how can this be? This is another, I don't know, but to me, it does not matter. Supernaturally, or technologically, I have no doubt this will happen. We read in verses 30 and 31 that He (The Son of Man) will be seen coming on the clouds of Heaven with power and glory, and the angels will sound the trumpet to call to gather the elect from the four winds and from Heaven.

This appears to me to fulfill the call for the Feast of Tabernacles with the trumpets. We are to assemble and make ready. The "elect," together with angels and the saints already in Heaven will prepare to clean the Church and gather the harvest of souls.

We are given more revelation of how and what will happen in verses 36 through 41. We see the signs and know that the end is near, but no one knows the exact time. However just as it was in the time of Noah, people will be doing people things and not paying attention or getting prepared. The flood came and the unprepared were swept away. This time there may be two in a field. One will be taken and the other left. The same for women doing their work. One will be taken and the other left behind.

Believers may be taken out before the worst of the worst is over, but it seems that no one will be exempt from some suffering and difficult times. Our pastors and Christian leaders must get this message out to help the people prepare. We must be prepared for whatever happens. There will be difficulty in getting food and water and the things we take for granted today, at least in the more developed countries. Perhaps those who are accustomed to difficult living and the lack of conveniences for everything will be the most able to survive the losses.

Verse 29 gives me some confusion. It reads that "after the distress of those days the sun will be darkened, and the moon will not give its light; the stars will fall from the sky, and the heavenly bodies will be shaken." How might it happen that we see neither the sun nor the moon? We have seen meteor showers which we have called shooting stars, or such, but what is going to cause us to see neither the sun nor the moon and create such darkness?

The only thing I can think of is what happens with severe volcanic eruptions. When and where the heavy ash hovers over the earth, the sky is blocked out day and night. If there are several eruptions, the earth could essentially be blackened out until the ash begins to fall out. This could at least happen for several days and would certainly add more distress and colder temperatures. If this happens "after the distress of those days," what we are going to have is more severe distress.

Come to a relationship with Jesus Christ now, and before it is too late.

Even though I do not believe Christians (and Jews) will avoid all distress and tribulation, Jesus did say in verse 22 "for the sake of the elect those days will be shortened."

Considering the totality of chapter 24, we know that we have seen many of the "signs" throughout the years, but in verse 33 Jesus explained that when all of these signs come, that is when the beginning of the end will begin. Many, most, and very easily all of the "signs" could manifest themselves now or very soon.

C. SOME THOUGHTS ON THE RAPTURE AND ITS TIMING.

All I have just written leads me to believe there will come a time when the true believers will be taken out from terrible times. Jesus said as much in His Olivet Discourse. The question remains, however, when will that occur? There are verses supporting the idea of an "imminent" removal when real trouble begins, commonly called "pretrib," However, there is to be a time for cleansing, and selecting, and the ingathering of new believers. Who would remain to help with the work and the "harvest?"

Let's look at some of the passages in the Bible which relate to the issue. In Revelation 13:5-7, we learn:

> The beast was given a mouth to utter proud words and blasphemies and to exercise its *authority for forty-two months.* ⁶It opened its mouth to blaspheme God, and to slander his name and his dwelling place and those who live in heaven. ⁷It was given *power to wage war against God's holy people and to conquer them. And it was given authority over every tribe, people, language and nation.* (Emphasis added)

This indicates that the "beast," (i.e. "The anti-Christ") will have power over God's people for three-and-a-half years.

Again, in Daniel 7:25, we read, "He will speak against the Most High and oppress his holy people and try to change the set times and the laws. The holy people will be delivered into his hands for a time, times and half a time." When the Bible speaks of a time, times and a half a time, it is saying three-and-a-half years. A time is one year, times is two years, and half a time is a half year.

In Daniel 9, Daniel tells of the rebuilding of Jerusalem and the Temple even though it will be in the time of trouble. A leader will come to destroy them, and in verse 27 we read, "He will confirm a covenant with many for one 'seven.' In the middle of the 'seven' he will put an end to sacrifice and offering. And at the temple he will set up an abomination that causes desolation, until the end that is decreed is poured out on him."

There is to be an agreement to last for seven years, and during this time the Temple may be used. However, the agreement is broken after three-and-a-half years, and the Jewish use of the Temple ceases. It becomes the abomination of desolation which was referred to by Jesus in Matthew 24:15. The anti-Christ makes himself God and demands worship. The Temple is desecrated, and God begins pouring out His judgment.

I will quote one more passage from the Book of Daniel 12:1-4.

At that time Michael, the great prince who protects your people, will arise. There will be a time of distress such as has not happened from the beginning of nations until then. But at that time your people—everyone whose name is found written in the book—will be delivered. ²Multitudes who sleep in the dust of the earth will awake: some to everlasting life, others to shame and everlasting contempt. ³Those who are wise will shine like the brightness of the heavens, and those who lead many to righteousness, like the stars for ever and ever. ⁴*But you, Daniel, roll up and seal the words of the scroll until the time of the end. Many will go here and there to increase knowledge.* (Emphasis added.)

The time spoken of was when the anti-Christ is defeated. When Daniel gets this information, he is told to roll up his writing and seal the words until the time of the end. So, so far, we do not know at what point Christ will return unless it is when the anti-Christ is to be defeated, and Satan is to be cast out. Likewise, we cannot be certain when the Church and saints will be raptured. Whatever, Daniel was told to put away his scroll, as these things would not be known until the end of the age. I will do likewise. If Daniel did not or could not have the answers, how can I?

To say that all of this is mind-boggling is an understatement. The one thing I firmly believe is that there will be no rapture earlier than three-and-a-half years into the seven-year agreement. However, if this is when real tribulation and God's wrath begins to pour out, this could be the timing for what amounts to a pretrib rapture. Perhaps much of the first three-and-a-half years of the peace agreement could be very uncomfortable and dangerous for Christians, but then Jesus steps in to remove His saints before the real wrath of God and the anti-Christ begins.

Much of my confusion centers around the seven years. What does the seven-year period really refer to? If the seven years relates to the agreed time concerning use of the Temple, as mentioned in the Book of Daniel, then the real tribulation is to begin after three-and-a-half years. (See also Paul's second letter to the Thessalonians 2:1-4). The tribulation will only be for the next three-and-a-half years, not an additional seven years. During this period, whether three-and-a-half or seven years, Jesus is to return and defeat Satan and the other forces of evil. If the rapture of the dead in Christ and the living saints who are ready to attend the feast with Christ in the heavenlies occurs at the beginning of the second half of the seven-year agreement, that for me would be pretrib.

This reasoning is believable for me, although many questions remain unanswered. Will all "Christians" be cleansed and ready, or will many believers be left behind to help with the harvest of souls and be strengthened in their own faith? Will the Church or churches be cleansed and ready, or will many be apostate and left out? I not only do not have all of the answers, but also I do not have all the questions.

I still have some concern about why the doctrine of a rapture was not advocated by many theologians and leaders during the time from Paul's teachings until around 1830. Paul's messages to the Corinthians and the Thessalonians, Daniel's prophesies, John's Revelation, and some of Jesus's sayings do support the idea of a rapture of living believers, as well as the dead in Christ. These passages speak to me of a seven-year agreement of which there will be three-and-a-half years of tribulation. I have somehow missed the evidence of seven years of actual tribulation. Otherwise, I concur with many of today's Christian leaders, and Bible expositors who are convinced that believers who are still living and prepared will be instantaneously transformed into a glorified body and taken to heaven prior to the tribulation. I must say, I like the idea.

What is most important, however, is that I want to prepare myself to be acceptable for whatever God plans to do, and whenever He plans to do it. I will put my faith and trust in Jesus Christ, and His blood covenant He made for all Mankind who will believe in Him and follow His commandments. He is my mediator and advocate, and that gives me a sense of security. While I do like the idea of a rapture, I just want to be ready. The timing is of little concern for me.

To each of you, I urge you to watch for the signs, stay alert, and get prepared. Understand and believe in who Jesus was, is, and what He did for us. Keep the faith. May the grace of God fall on each of us as underserving sinners.

A few events over the past years seem to be fulfilling end-time prophecies. The Jews now have a homeland, they have returned to Jerusalem, and through the courage of President Donald Trump, Jerusalem is now recognized as the Capital of Israel by the United States and many other countries. Stay alert. Be ready for whatever and whenever God decides it is time for Jesus to return. I hope to have my soul ready for anything. I urge you to do the same.

D. WHAT ABOUT AMERICA?

In Revelation 17:4-5, we read, The woman was dressed in purple and scarlet, and was glittering with gold, precious stones and pearls. She held a golden cup in her hand, filled with abominable things and the filth of her adulteries. ⁵The name written on her forehead was a

Mystery:

babylon the great

the mother of prostitutes

and of the abominations of the earth.

Is America the "Mystery Babylon?" Could it be New York City? Reading the description in chapters 17, 18, and 19, it could be either, although I have heard arguments that the Middle East with all of its excesses could fit the description. However, America seems to make more sense, to me. Picture John seeing all of the revelations. He was seeing things he had no idea or knowledge about. These could be the locust which could be helicopters and large hailstones which could be bombs. Likewise, America was not known in those days and would be a "mystery." Wherever this abominable mystery place might be, it is going to be destroyed when the time for judgment comes.

Consider what America started out to be, became, and has now become. In a nutshell, America began with the planting of a cross at Cape May at the mouth of Chesapeake Bay when the English colonists first landed in North America in 1607. Those that came to Massachusetts came for freedom to worship God and Jesus Christ. From such beginnings, the country grew and was blessed. When America sought independence, the Declaration of Independence continued to reference God. Our Constitution was based on Judeo-Christian principles. Many of the legislated laws were based on biblical concepts, including such as the exemption of Church property from taxation, and the "Blue Sky laws."

While the country's growth and rise in power was far from perfect, this country was *blessed* as no other society has ever been. By the latter part of the nineteenth century, America had become the world's leading economic power, and by the midtwentieth century, its currency had become the preferred currency for the world. The rest of the world traded with America, and it became enormously strong—economically and militarily.

What had been a successful nation and world leader, it began losing its spiritual, moral, and ethical sense of direction. Beginning in the 1930s, the Humanist movement began its crusade to remove any idea of a God, divine power, and biblical teachings from the public domain. Over the past eighty or ninety years, America has been turned upside down by the efforts of this and other relatively small, but very vocal, groups. What was good is now bad. What was right is now wrong. Christian teachings have been systematically removed from schools, government, and society in general. Our teachings and directions must not be offensive to anyone. Well, for what it is worth, I have been offended by all of this activity.

The sexual revolution has caused unintended consequences. (Disasters might be more appropriate.) Consider, for example, the breakup of so many families, the vast number of fatherless children, the killing of perhaps as many as seventy million unborn babies for birth control, and now the revelation that often the body parts are harvested and sold for profit. We also see the spread of so many sexually transmitted diseases. Most recently, the idea of same-sex "marriages" has been approved. Our chief executive celebrated the Supreme Court's approval with his approval by illuminating the people's house, the White House, with rainbow colors. In a syndicated editorial by Thomas Sowell on June 30, 2015, he included the decision in his article entitled, "Supreme Court Disasters."

Giving a bit more credit to Thomas Sowell, whose editorials I cannot remember ever disagreeing with, he wrote on July 21, 2015: "A Historic Catastrophe." In it, he classified the recent proposed deal with Iran, as a "worst ever." Indeed, it could be the worst political blunder in the history of civilization. The Trump administration reversed it, but now the Biden administration is working to restore it.

To such thoughts, I would like to add that the "deal" punctuates how far America is going in the abandonment of Israel. It is not by just this latest "deal," but it is evident by so many of our more recent slights and insulting treatment of Israel. We need to be reminded of God's promise to Abraham: "I will bless those who bless you, and *whoever curses you I will curse*; and all peoples on earth will be blessed through you." (Emphasis added). Genesis 12:3.

America should reflect back to 1948, when President Harry Truman was a really significant factor in the establishment of Israel. As a nation,

America has been a friend and ally with Israel for many years. There is evidence by various negative coincidences affecting America, which coincide with times when America has made negative proposals which would adversely affect Israel.

America's excessive national debt is another inexcusable evil. America is now bankrupt, and the excesses have and will affect the entire world.

Morally, America is bankrupt. Consider our movie and the pornographic industries. I am old enough to remember when the movie industry operated by a code which prohibited unmarried, opposite sex couples from being filmed in bed together. So, in 1943, when a new starlet, Jane Russell, who could warm up any man, got into bed with the male star to help him combat a chill (medicinal purposes), viewers were shocked. Well, the rest is history. Today, anything goes. While the old code was perhaps overly restrictive, what is allowed today seems to have swung too far in the other direction. Sex, drugs, violence, and perversion are all now glorified.

With all of the evil in America's society these days, it should not be too shocking that the ayatollahs in Iran, etc., refer to America as the "Great Satan." However, that tag for America is a bit too much from them. Such is comparable to the kettle calling the pot—black.

I will not elaborate more on these points at this time, but will refer you to Appendix B, which is an opinion I wrote in late 1993. It can speak for itself, but I will add that the situation has only gotten worse, not better.

Many of our churches and denominations are adopting these politically correct ways, and they are becoming absolutely apostate. It is time for the churches to unite and fight all of the "political and biblical *In*correctness."

How far will God allow these abominations to continue? America got a warning on September 11, 2001, when the protective hand of God was lifted, and our towers representing our world economic power were knocked down. Also, the Pentagon, the emblem of our military power, was also hit.

If there was any repentance as a Nation, it was short-lived, and we have continued to thumb our noses at God. Our national leadership immediately quoted Isaiah 9:10, "The bricks have fallen down, but we will rebuild with dressed stone; the fig trees have been felled, but we will replace them with cedars." Had they read the rest of the passage, they would have noticed that this arrogance brought destructive judgment on Israel. But no, we have now replaced the towers with one taller than the ones that were knocked down. They even replaced a sycamore tree at ground zero with a stronger evergreen tree, although I understand it has since died.

For more, and really excellent information about this subject, I refer the reader to two books by Rabbi Jonathan Cahn. (A Messianic Jew). They are *The Harbinger* and *The Mystery of the Shemitah*. Information about these publications will be found in Appendix A.

There is no way I can say what will happen, how it will happen, or when something will happen, but God will not be mocked forever. It is abundantly clear, however, that America has turned its back on God. America's destruction could come from foreign enemies, internal enemies, or it could come from natural and/or supernatural disasters.

President Ronald Reagan once said something like: "If America ever ceases to be one nation under God, it will become one nation gone under." This is happening, good people. I am afraid it is too late for real and effective repentance. However, and although, in the following scripture, God was speaking to Israel, nevertheless as adopted sons, or covenant partners through Jesus Christ, it would be a good idea for America and Christians to try to comply with 2 Chronicles 7:14, which tells us:

¹⁴If my people, who are called by my name, will humble them-selves and pray and seek my face and turn from their wicked

ways, then I will hear from heaven, and I will forgive their sin and will heal their land.

Indeed, His (adopted) people had better give it a try, and those who are now ready to become covenant partners and adopted sons (and daughters) need to join the effort.

Blessings to all, and may God have mercy on America and this world.
Understand your Christianity and Develop your Soul.
To GOD be the Glory! Amen!!

✝

†

EPILOGUE

Then Jesus came to them and said, "All authority in heaven and on earth has been given to me. Therefore, go and make disciples of all nations, baptizing them in the name of the Father and of the Son and of the Holy Spirit, and teaching them to obey everything I have commanded you. And surely, I am with you always, to the very end of the age."
(MATTHEW 28:18-20)

So much is going on in this world today. With the reduction in the number of Christians in America, and the absolute evil that is going in the world perpetrated by the Islamic State or the radical Islamic jihadists, I decided an epilogue to close out the book would be in order.

As we can read from the quoted scripture above, our God is with us to the end. Therefore, do not lose hope, Christians. God is still sovereign. Our God reigns. Although in America the percentage of the population identifying as Christian has diminished somewhat, the same is not true for the world at large.

It is also discouraging to witness all the evil on display throughout the world whether from ISIS, or drug cartels, or whatever. In the free world, the West, and in America, we see the utter disregard of God's commandments for civilized society as found in the Bible. Elsewhere, we are witnessing the absolute demonic evil perpetrated by the radical elements of Islam intent on world domination through what they call Jihad. They use terror as their primary method for conquest. They slaughter, mutilate, rape, and enslave innocent people, primarily non-Muslims, but also other Muslims who do not believe the same way as the radical Jihadists.

When Christians challenge the horror of radical Jihad, the response is: What about the Crusades? Well, what about them? There is no moral equivalency. Islamic Jihad for world domination began with their Prophet around AD 620. The purpose and methods were the same then as today. Over the past 1,400 years there have been over 500 attacks against civilization and the Christian world. Between AD 1080 and AD 1260 there were perhaps 14 crusades. The main purposes for the crusades were to restore Christianity and rescue people taken as slaves.

For a time, the Muslims essentially controlled the **Mediterranean** Sea and all commerce and trade among the adjoining countries. With all of their pirating such commerce all but stopped. In the early 1800s, President Thomas Jefferson increased an American Navy to fight the pirates and help free United States merchant seamen who had been enslaved.

It is time for the free world to again free the world of such evil.

I have no doubt that a large majority of believers in Islam do not openly support or participate in radical Jihad. However, if that is true, then why do they not make some effort to stop the terrorism? Consider also the apparent disenfranchisement of women, the stoning of women, and the killing of homosexuals. The silence of the alleged majority is deafening. Is it the result of belief, toleration, or cowardice?

Christians also face other opponents of Christianity. Christians are increasingly attacked by atheists, humanists, educators, those in control of public media, and even their own government. Anti-Christians seek to take control of our constitutional freedoms, and especially free speech. They seek to eliminate debate and disagreement related to their anti-Christian beliefs.

They seek to control our language by creating "hate speech." This can be anything that might offend anyone or their ideas. Words of hope and truth from the Gospel could become prohibited when such are offensive to someone in a politically protected group. The situation is closer than most people are aware. It is time to wake up and push back to stop this menace and the loss of our freedoms.

At the 1964 Republican National Convention, Senator Barry Goldwater—the eventual nominee for president in that year made a statement which was heard mostly negatively. What he said was true and is perhaps more needed and appropriate for today. He said, "Extremism in defense of liberty is no vice, and moderation in pursuit of justice is no virtue." Undoubtedly Christians must pick up the pace to defend our liberty and promote and maintain justice. However, such action must not be intolerant as the opponents of Christianity have been. Christians must be tolerant and open to debate but without violence. The Christian beliefs have eternal value and can stand up against anything in open and honest debate and dialogue. It must be done with love, respect, and toleration, but it need not fold or cease in response to intolerance and violence from opponents.

With all that is going on in the world, it is imperative that Christian clergy in all denominations speak up and out. Tell your "flock" what is going on in the world and what the Bible truly says. Do not fear teaching and preaching about end-time prophesies. Some people may not want to hear it, but you must help them prepare spiritually, mentally, and physically.

The clergy are the watchmen that have been assigned, or volunteered, to be the "watchmen on the walls." They will be held accountable for losses when they see the enemy and fail to sound the alarm. See, for example, Ezekiel 33:3-6, and 1 Timothy 4:13-16.

I have to wonder just how prepared many of our churches are for the return of Jesus. In the first three chapters of the Book of Revelation, Jesus is speaking to John and gives John messages to give to the seven churches in Asia Minor. Each message revealed the good and bad about each church. This tells me that if Jesus knew the good and bad of each church in those days, He knows what each church is doing in these days. We can be sure God is not pleased with apostasy and political correctness in His church. If pastors recognize such under their supervision, it is time to clean house and get prepared. Jesus will return for a pure bride. Only five of the ten virgins were prepared when the bridegroom came.

One final admonition to the clergy on this issue: Do not scoff or mock any clergy who are helping their "flock" to prepare.

I want to close with a final suggestion. I encourage each to read the attachments. Attachment B relates to how God and biblical principles are being systematically removed from our public discourse and education system, resulting in our world being turned topsy-turvy with evil being hailed as good and what was good being denounced as evil. Keep in mind that the opinion was written concerning the situation in 1992 and 1993. The times, they are changing.

It is past time for Christians to rise up and push back. Remember, the vigorous pursuit of liberty, freedom, and the spread of the Gospel of Jesus Christ is no vice. Sitting back and just watching the loss of these precious things is no virtue.

Stand up and step in, Christian. To God be the glory. Amen!

P.S. As a final note, I want to thank each reader for taking the time to read this book. If you have learned from it and been strengthened in your faith, then I urge you to share the book or at least tell others about it. I especially urge you to share the contents of this book with your teenagers, and certainly if they will soon be leaving home for a secular university. It can be life-changing for them.

The book is available in print or electronically. Encourage your local Churches, libraries and schools to make it available to the public.

Unfortunately, at my age and condition, I will not be going about attempting to carry out the "great commission," but I can participate by helping spread the "word" via this book. If you have been blessed, you can help by encouraging your friends in person or on your social media to get a copy or maybe join in a group study.

Finally, it would be very helpful, if you would give some feedback to the source of your purchase and provide a good rating.

My thanks and appreciation. J. William Howerton

✝

† NOTES

PREFACE

1. Colson, Charles, *Loving God,* (Zondervan Publishing House, 1983), 26-37.
2. Ibid. 35. Colson was quoting from Alexander Solzhenitsyn, *Gulag Archipelago II* (New York: Harper and Row. 1974), 613-15.
3. Nash, Ogden, *Selected Verse,* (The Modern Library, Random House, 1945), 30.

CHAPTER 1. WHY THIS BOOK

1. Colson, Charles, *The Faith,* (Zondervan, 2008), 58.
2. Ibid. 59.

CHAPTER 2. THE HOLY BIBLE

1. Mahoney, Timothy P., with Steven Law *Patterns of Evidence—The Exodus,* (Thinking Man's Media, 2015). This information is for the book. The movie was shown January 19, 2015, and is available on DVD.
2. McDowell, Josh, *Evidence That Demands a Verdict,* (Campus Crusade for Christ, Inc., 1972)
3. Geva, Hillel, Editor, *Ancient Jerusalem Revealed,* (Israel Exploration Society, 1974). ISBN 965-221-021-8.

4. Bartlett, Clarence, *As a Lawyer Sees Jesus,* (New Life, a Division of Standard Publishing, 1960).

CHAPTER 6. THE HOLY SPIRIT

1. Slosser, Bob, *Miracle in Darien,* (Bridge-Logos Publishers, 1980).
2. Lewis, C. S., *The Screwtape Letters,* (Revised Paperback Edition, 1982, McMillian Publishing Company, ISBN 0-02-086740-9).
3. Thomas, Major W. Ian, *The Saving Life of Christ,* (Zondervan Publishing House, 1961), 17-18.

†

APPENDIX A

SUGGESTED READING

The books listed below are listed by writer, and not for a specific category or purpose. Some will be for guidance, some for study aids, and some for general moral and Christian enlightenment and inspiration.

Kay Arthur: *Lord, Where Are You When Bad Things Happen?*, *How To Study Your Bible*, Consider also *The International Inductive Study Bible*, and *Heaven, Hell and Life after Death*, with Bob and Diane Vereen, and a recent pamphlet, *America on the Edge*, which ties in closely with chapter 8 and appendix B.

William J. Bennett: *The Book of Virtues*, *The Moral Compass*, and *Our Sacred Honor*

Mark Biltz: *God's Day Timer*

Jonathan Cahn: *The Harbinger*, *The Mystery of the Shemitah*, *The Paradigm*, *The Oracle*, and *The Book of Mysteries*

Ben Carson: *One Nation*

Charles Colson: *The Faith*, *The Christian in Today's Culture*, *A Dangerous Grace*, *How Now Shall We Live? Born Again*, and *Loving God*

Dinesh D'Souza: *What's So Great About Christianity?*

Billy Graham: *The Holy Spirit, Just as I Am, Angels, God's Secret Agents, Living as a Christian, Approaching Hoofbeats, Storm Warning, The Journey,* and *The Reason for My Hope*

Franklin Graham: *The Name,* and *Billy Graham in Quotes*

John Hagee: *Four Blood Moons*

William Hoenig: *Eye to Eye*

David Kupelian: *The Marketing of Evil*

C. S. Lewis: *Mere Christianity* and *The Screwtape Letters*

Josh McDowell: *Right From Wrong, More Than A Carpenter, A Ready Defense, Evidence That Demands A Verdict,* and *The New Evidence*

Nancy Pearcey and Charles B. Thaxton: *The Soul of Science and Natural Philosophy*

Joel Richardson: *The Islamic AntiChrist,* and *When A Jew Rules The World*

Pat Robertson: *The New World Order, The End of the Age,* and *Shout it from the Housetops*

Ian Thomas: *The Saving Life of Christ*

Ravi Zacharis: *Can Man Live Without God*

A list such as this could be endless. Good Christian books by good Christian authors will help you in your Christian growth.

†

APPENDIX B

In this appendix is a copy of a concurring opinion I wrote in 1993. The first page is the caption, and I have omitted the brief opinion of the court, merely affirming a summary judgment.

The action was brought by three families in Northern Kentucky seeking to have the Commonwealth provide funding to allow them to send their children to private or Christian schools. The case was dismissed by the trial court by Summary Judgment. A Summary Judgment is authorized when considering all of the allegations in a complaint, along with supporting affidavits or sworn testimony, the plaintiff cannot win as a matter of law. This was such a case, and on appeal, our court had no choice but to affirm the trial court's judgment.

The opinion added nothing to the body of law concerning Summary Judgments, so, therefore, there was no reason to publish it, and it was so designated.

I nevertheless took the opportunity to unleash some of my personal feelings about the situation which was happening in this country. It will be apparent that I definitely did have serious concerns, and perhaps frustrations.

I will let the opinion speak for itself but will urge you to think as you read it, just how much farther America has gone downhill since

169

1993. It is a crying shame, but what was The Light and the Glory for the World, or That Shining Light on a Hill, America is simply not what it used to be.

Included in the opinion are appropriate comments from a speech delivered by Charles Colson, in September 1993, when he accepted the "Templeton Prize for Progress in Religion." Transcription was made from a tape recording of the speech.

I hope each reader will be blessed by Colson's comments and receive other benefits and enlightenment from the totality of the opinion. Then ask yourself: Can America ever turn its ship of state around without her citizens first turning to God and enlisting His aid?

Commonwealth Of Kentucky
Court Of Appeals

NO. 92-CA-002418-MR

RAYMOND C. MILLER AND
ANN W. MILLER,
RAMONDA G. MILLER,
KENDRA A. MILLER,
JOSEPH A. MILLER, AND
MICHAEL A. MILLER,
REPRESENTED BY THEIR PARENTS
AND NEXT FRIENDS;

MICHAEL MARTIN AND JO MARTIN,
MICHAEL MARTIN, JR.,
CARLEY MARTIN, MATTHEW MARTIN
AND JOANNA MARTIN,
REPRESENTED BY THEIR PARENTS
AND NEXT FRIENDS;

ROY THOMPSON AND PEGGY THOMPSON,
CARRIE THOMPSON, AARON THOMPSON,
TARA THOMPSON, SETH THOMPSON AND
EVA THOMPSON, REPRESENTED BY
THEIR PARENTS AND NEXT FRIENDS   APPELLANTS

v.   APPEAL FROM FRANKLIN CIRCUIT COURT
            HONORABLE ROGER L. CRITTENDEN, JUDGE
               CIVIL ACTION NO. 92-CI-00021

BRERETON C. JONES, GOVERNOR,
COMMONWEALTH OF KENTUCKY;
JOHN STEPHENSON, SUPERINTENDENT
OF PUBLIC INSTRUCTION;
THOMAS C. BOYNSEN, COMMISSIONER
OF EDUCATION; FRANCES JONES MILLS,
STATE TREASURER; JOHN A. ROSE,
PRESIDENT PRO TEMPORE OF THE SENATE;
AND DONALD J. BLANFORD, MEMBER OF
THE HOUSE OF REPRESENTATIVES   APPELLEES

UNDERSTANDING GOD'S CONTRACTS WITH MANKIND

HOWERTON, JUDGE, CONCURS IN RESULT AND FILES SEPARATE OPINION.

HOWERTON, JUDGE, CONCURRING. I concur with the result reached by
the majority, but I write separately to express my concern for
the issues and problems raised by the appellants' complaint.
They received less than their "full day in court," and they
deserve to know that their cause is understood. It is common
knowledge that many parents in Kentucky and throughout the United

States would provide something other than public education for
their children if they could. People are concerned with the
quality of education their children receive, the lack of
discipline and a good learning environment in many public
schools, and the types of values their children are receiving. I
cannot simply concur and remain silent when all around me I see
our society crumbling, and when I believe our public education
system is at least a big part of the problem.

Any criticism contained in this opinion is not directed
to any individual educator, school board member, executive, or
legislator. Also, public education is certainly not the sole
cause of our troubles. For one thing, it is not the sole source
of learning. We learn from life and all we are exposed to.
Nevertheless, education is an important part in the development
of values and social conduct. As Plato pointed out in The
Republic, "The direction in which education starts a man will
determine his future life." The way we train our children today
will determine the way our country goes tomorrow.

Although the appellants' case was dismissed by summary
judgment, the appellees should not take the dismissal as any

reason to ignore the problem. According to Rose v. Council for Better Education, Inc., Ky., 790 S.W.2d 186 (1989), the establishment, maintenance, and funding of an efficient system of common schools is the sole responsibility of the legislature. However, the governor must also take a leadership role, if any changes are likely to happen. The problems will not simply go away, and indeed it may take several generations to correct them, if they are correctable. My objective is certainly not to harm public education, and any comment I make will be intended to possibly improve it.

In my opinion, the underlying problems with public education began approximately 60 years ago. However, it was not until approximately 30 years ago, when schools began the systematic removal or censorship of anything based on Judeo-Christian principles, that we really hit the skids. Unless someone has been snuggled up with Rip Van Winkle in Sleepy Hollow for the past 20 years, there is no way one can fail to see what results this censorship has brought.

In this concurrence, I will first consider some of the costs caused by the loss of morality in our society and the loss of a good learning environment in our schools. I will then attempt to identify some of the root causes which must be considered if improvement is to come. Next, I will identify some of what we formerly believed in compared to what is now taught, and finally, we may be able to make some generalizations which might be a basis for reversing our troubles.

In the western industrialized world, we are now number one in violent crime, number one in teenage pregnancies, number

2

one in divorce, and number one in illiteracy. Sexually-transmitted diseases are up, and SAT scores are down. With the breakup of so many families, so many immature parents, the loss of discipline, the lack of respect for anything and everyone (including self), and the idea that nothing is right or wrong, what else should we expect?

At the time of this writing, congress is considering a new crime bill calling for an additional expenditure of 20 billion dollars. This is to provide more police officers and more prison space. During the past 20 years, our prison population has risen from approximately 200,000 to 900,000 inmates. Current cost for incarceration of criminals is over 70 billion dollars. Where will it end? We spend another 20 billion dollars or more on welfare for teenage mothers. What kind of citizens will their children become? Another 5 billion dollars, more or less, is spent in the treatment of AIDS, and this figure will only increase. Approximately 90 percent of the AIDS cases are directly related to sexual misconduct or illegal drug activity. Much of our health care costs are directly related to misbehavior; for example, violence, drunkenness, drug abuse, sexual diseases, and babies having babies, to name a few. Any escalation in such conduct with universal health care may bankrupt this country. How can we possibly get out of debt, if behavior does not improve? Much of our federal expenditures go for the cost of immoral behavior, and when we add state and local government costs and insurance costs, we are wasting far too much of our gross national product.

3

APPENDIX B

In 1983, the National Commission on Excellence in
Education submitted a report entitled "A Nation at Risk: The
Imperative for Educational Reform." At page 11, we read, "For
the first time in the history of our country, the educational
skills of one generation will not surpass, will not equal, will
not even approach, those of their parents." The report went on
to indicate that although more people were now better educated,
the average graduate was not as well-educated as the average
graduate of 25 years earlier. What percent of our people are
functionally illiterate now, and how much worse will it get?

How did we get into this condition? For me, one of the
most concise, precise, and correct explanations was given in a
speech delivered at the University of Chicago on September 2,
1993, by Charles Colson. His speech was delivered as part of his
acceptance of the 1993 "Templeton Award," which is given for
progress in religion. The award is not confined to any
particular religion, and it was for Colson's work with Prison
Fellowship. The value of the award exceeded 1 million dollars,
and the money was used to endow Prison Fellowship. In the
speech, Colson said:[1]

> Four great myths define our times. The four
> horsemen of the present Apocalypse.
>
> The first myth is the goodness of man,
> and the first horseman rails against heaven

---

[1] Transcribed from a tape recording.

> with the presumptuous question, "Why do bad
> things happen to good people?" He multiplies
> evil by denying its existence. . . . It
> dismisses responsibility as the teachings of
> a darker age. It can excuse any crime,
> because it can always blame something else--a
> sickness of society or a sickness of the
> mind. One writer has called the modern age,
> the golden age of exoneration.

This first myth is by no means new. The philosophical debate on

the nature of man has gone on for centuries. More recently,

however, we have tended to excuse misbehavior and failed to hold

people accountable for their actions because of environmental

factors. I remember seeing the musical "West Side Story" around

1960. In one of the scenes, some gang members were taunting a

policeman named Officer Krupke. The dialogue involved whether

the boys were bad or good, and one finally said, "Yeah, I'm

depraved on account I'm deprived."

Colson continued:

> The second myth of modernity is the
> promise of coming Utopia, and the second
> horseman arrives with sword and slaughter.
> This is the myth that human nature can be
> perfected by government. . . . The
> political illusion still deceives, whether
> it's called the great society, the new
> covenant, or the new world order. In each
> case it promises government solutions to the
> deepest needs for security, peace, and
> meaning in the human heart.

> The third myth is the relativity of moral
> values, and the third horseman sows chaos and
> confusion. This myth obscures the dividing
> line between good and evil, noble and base.
> . . . When a society abandons its
> transcendent values, each individual's moral
> vision becomes purely personal and finally
> equal. Society becomes merely the sum total
> of individual preferences, and since no
> preference is more preferable, anything that
> can be dared will be permitted. . . . Moral
> neutrality slips into moral relativism.
> Tolerance substitutes for truth, indifference

5

for religious conviction, and in the end,
confusion undercuts all of our creeds.

The fourth modern myth is radical
individualism, and the fourth horseman brings
excess and isolation. This myth dismisses
the importance of family, church, and
community; denies the value of sacrifice; and
elevates individual rights and pleasures as
the ultimate social value.

Colson further explains and elaborates on the four myths as

follows:

My friends, crime is a mirror of a
community's moral state, and a society cannot
long survive if the demands of human dignity
are not written on our hearts. No number of
police can enforce order; no threat of
punishment can create it. Crime and violence
frustrate every political answer, because
there can be no solution apart from character
and creed. But relativism and individualism
have undermined the traditional beliefs that
once formed our character and defined our
creed.

. . .

. . . Modernity was once judged by the
heights of its aspirations. Today it must be
judged by the depth of its decadence, and
that decadence tragically has marked the West
most deeply. That makes it imperative for
all of us, from whatever part of the world we
come, from whatever faith community, to
understand the struggle that is going on
today for the heart and soul of Western
civilization.

. . .

Christian conviction also shapes personal
virtue--the moral imperative to be good. It
subdues an obstinate will. It ties a tether
to self-interest and violence. . . .

This then, my friends, is the lesson of
the centuries, that ordered liberty is one of
faith's triumphs; and yet, Western and
cultural political elites seem blinded by
modernity's myths to the historic civilizing
role of the Christian faith. In the guise of
pluralism and tolerance, they have set about
to exile religion from our common life. They

6

use the power of the media and the law like
steel wool to scrub public debates and public
places bare of religious ideas and symbols.
But what is left is sterile, featureless,
cold. These elites seek freedom without
self-restraint, liberty without standards,
but they find instead, the revenge of
offended absolutes.

Courts strike down even perfunctory
prayers, and then we are surprised that
schools, bristling with barbed wire, look
more like prisons than prisons do.
Universities reject the very idea of truth
and we are shocked when the best and
brightest of their graduates loot and betray.
Celebrities mock the traditional family, even
revile it as a form of slavery and we're
appalled at the human tragedy of broken homes
and millions of unwed mothers. . . .

C. S. Lewis described this irony a
generation ago. "We laugh at honor," he
said, "and we are shocked to find traitors in
our midst. We castrate and bid the geldings
be fruitful." A generation of cultural
leaders wants to live off the spiritual
capital of its inheritance, while denigrating
the ideals of its ancestors. It slanders a
treasure it no longer values; it celebrates
its liberation when it ought to be trembling
for its very future.

. . .

This coming cultural tyranny is already
casting its shadow across university campuses
where repressive speech codes stifle free
debate; across courthouses and legislatures
where officials are hunting down and purging
every religious symbol; across network news
rooms and board rooms where nothing is
censored except traditional belief. Our
modern elites speak of enlightened
columnists, while preparing shackles for
those who disagree. . . . And so,
paradoxically, at the very moment so much of
the rest of the world is reaching out for the
Western liberal ideas, the West itself
beguiled by the myths of modernity is
undermining the very foundation of those
ideals. This is irony without humor; farce
without joy. Western elites are carefully
separating the wheat from the chaff and
keeping the chaff. They are performing a
modern miracle of turning wine into water.

7

APPENDIX B

> . . . I say to my compatriots in the West
> that we bear a particular responsibility for
> modernity's myths have found fertile soil in
> our lands and we have offered haven to the
> four horsemen who trampled the dreams and
> hopes of men everywhere. As the world looks
> to us, let us summon up our courage to
> challenge our comfortable assumptions, to
> scrutinize the effect we are having on our
> global neighbors, and then to recover that
> which has been the very soul and conscience
> of our civilization.

The "myths" are what is being taught, what is publicly
presented as truth, and what we are exposed to every day in
almost every facet of life, including many modern "Christian"
churches. The debate of whether there is a supernatural force
which created the universe and maintains some order in it, or
whether everything just somehow happened and is all natural, has
gone on for years. The so-called "enlightenment period" began in
the 18th Century, and for the most part, the "enlightened"
philosophers denied the supernatural. Mankind was supreme and
man was on his own. In a sense, man could be his own god. This
is "humanism," "naturalism," and "new age" theory, but there is
nothing really new about it. In the Genesis story of Eve's
temptation by the serpent, we are given metaphorically the big
idea which all humans must confront, that is, that we can be like
God.

At the time this country was founded, however, America
was made up of a religious people, predominantly Christian, and
our founders created a government based on Greco-Roman-Christian,
and European traditions, or "the wisdom of the West", which had
developed over many centuries. Our founders took what was good
and avoided what was bad. The four myths identified by Colson
were not yet part of our culture.

8

179

Rector, etc., of Holy Trinity Church v. United States,
143 U.S. 457, 12 S.Ct. 511 (1892), is an unusual case which
traces and summarizes much of the religious heritage of our
country. The case decided that legislation prohibiting the
bringing of aliens to the United States for purposes of
employment did not apply to the bringing of a new pastor from
England to serve as rector of Holy Trinity Church. In doing so,
the unanimous opinion of the U. S. Supreme Court based its
decision in part on the fact that Americans are a religious
people and that the Court should not impute to any legislation a
purpose against religion.

Beginning at 12 S. Ct. 514, the opinion traces and
documents our religious (Christian) roots from Columbus'
commission to the more contemporary writings and cases. It cited
compacts and grants, the Declaration of Independence, and the
constitutions of several states. Although it did not cite the
Kentucky Constitution, it should be noted that its beginning and
ending read as follows:

> We, the people of the Commonwealth of
> Kentucky, grateful to Almighty God for the
> civil, political and religious liberties we
> enjoy, and invoking the continuance of these
> blessings, do ordain and establish this
> Constitution.
>
>   . . .
>
> Done at Frankfort this twenty-eighth day
> of September, in the year of our Lord one
> thousand eight hundred and ninety-one, and in
> the one hundredth year of the Commonwealth.

We have come a long way since 1892, but there can be no
doubt that America was founded on Biblical principles. They were
the basis for our Constitution, and such things as three branches

9

of government, separation of powers, the exemption of Sundays in counting time, tax exemptions for church property, and the oath given to witnesses.

At this point, it might be well to give a few quotes of some of our founders concerning their beliefs and the need for religion and morality in a democracy. In George Washington's Farewell Address,[2] he said:

> Here, perhaps, I ought to stop.--But a solicitude for your welfare, which cannot end but with my life, and the apprehension of danger, natural to that solicitude, urge me . . . to recommend to your frequent review, some sentiments; which are the result of much reflection, of no inconsiderable observation and which appear to me all important to the permanency of your felicity as a People. These will be offered to you with the more freedom, as . . . disinterested warnings of a parting friend, who can possibly have no personal motive to bias his counsel.
>
> . . .
>
> Of all the dispositions and habits, which lead to political prosperity, Religion, and Morality are indispensable supports.--In vain would that man claim the tribute of Patriotism, who should labor to subvert these great pillars of human happiness, these firmest props of the duties of Men and Citizens.--The mere Politician, equally with the pious man, ought to respect and to cherish them.--A volume could not trace all their connexions with private and public felicity.--Let it simply be asked where is the security for property, for reputation, for life, if the sense of religious obligation <u>desert</u> the oaths, which are the instruments of investigation in Courts of Justice? And let us with caution indulge the supposition, that morality can be maintained without religion.--Whatever may be conceded to the influence of refined education on minds of peculiar structure--reason and

---

[2] "Washington's Farewell Address (1796)," 43 <u>The Harvard Classics, American Historical Documents 1000-1904</u>, 252, 260, (1910).

10

experience both forbid us to expect, that national morality can prevail in exclusion of religious principle.

Benjamin Franklin, the venerable, 81-year-old elder statesman got the deadlocked Constitutional Convention back on track when he quietly said:[3]

> In the beginning of the contest with Britain, when we were sensible of danger, we had daily prayers in this room for Divine protection. Our prayers, Sir, were heard, and they were graciously answered. All of us who were engaged in the struggle must have observed frequent instances of a superintending Providence in our favor. . . . And have we now forgotten this powerful Friend? Or do we imagine we no longer need His assistance?

> I have lived, Sir, a long time, and the longer I live, the more convincing proofs I see of this truth: "that God governs in the affairs of man." And if a sparrow cannot fall to the ground without His notice, is it probable that an empire can rise without His aid?

> We have been assured, Sir, in the Sacred Writings that except the Lord build the house, they labor in vain that build it. I firmly believe this. I also believe that, without His concurring aid, we shall succeed in this political building no better than the builders of Babel; we shall be divided by our little, partial local interests; our projects will be confounded; and we ourselves shall become a reproach and a byword down to future ages. And what is worse, mankind may hereafter, from this unfortunate instance, despair of establishing government by human wisdom and leave it to chance, war, or conquest.

> I therefore beg leave to move that, henceforth, prayers imploring the assistance of Heaven and its blessing on our deliberation be held in this assembly every morning before we proceed to business.

---

[3] P. Marshall and D. Manuel, <u>The Light and the Glory</u>, 342-343 (1977).

11

APPENDIX B

Thomas Jefferson is frequently presented as a deist or secularist. However, Jefferson said, "My views are very different from that anti-Christian system imputed to me by those who know nothing of my opinions. To the corruptions of Christianity I am indeed, opposed, but not to the genuine precepts of Jesus himself. I am a Christian . . . ." He further stated, "The Christian religion . . . is a religion of all others most friendly to liberty, science and the freest expressions of the human mind."[4]

We have also heard how Jefferson cut all of the sayings of Jesus from the Gospels. Indeed, he did, at least four times. They were removed from translations in the Greek, Latin, French, and English. He pasted them in a book with his own writings, intending them to be used to explain the teachings to the Indians. In 1904, the 57th Congress ordered 9,000 copies published, 6,000 for the house and 3,000 for the senate. The title was, "The Life and Morals of Jesus of Nazareth by Thomas Jefferson."[5] The document was accompanied by an introduction by the librarian of congress.

One would be hard put to find any of the foregoing quotes, or similar quotes from such founders as Adams, Madison, or Mason, in school textbooks. I am not aware of any court decision which has directed the removal or censorship of such information from our school children, but the removal has been

---

[4] Beliles, Thomas Jefferson and the Words of Jesus of Nazareth, Vol. 8, No. 4, The Providential Perspective, September 1993, at 1, 8.

[5] T. Jefferson, The Life and Morals of Jesus of Nazareth, (1904).

12

183

the result of the desire of some who have worked their way into leadership and can effectively control what books are published and purchased for use in public schools. The information provides history and civics or political science lessons, and it is not any more a promotion of a religion than what is found is a promotion of the religions of humanism and atheism. It would indeed seem to be an absolutely ludicrous argument for one to say that it is unconstitutional to quote the opinions and beliefs of those who wrote the Constitution.

In more recent times, we might also consider the thoughts of such citizens as Justice Louis Brandies and Judge Learned Hand. Justice Brandies wrote:[6]

> Democracy . . . demands continuous sacrifice by the individual and more exigent obedience to the moral law than any other form of government. . . . It is possible only where the process of perfecting the individual is pursued. . . . Hence the industrial struggle is essentially an affair of the Church and its imperative task.

Judge Learned Hand gave a speech in 1944 during "I Am an American Day," in which he said:[7]

> I often wonder whether we do not rest our hopes too much upon constitutions, upon laws and upon courts. These are false hopes; believe me, these are false hopes. Liberty lies in the hearts of men and women; when it dies there, no constitution, no law, no court can save it; no constitution, no law, no court can even do much to help it. . . . And what is this liberty which must lie in the hearts of men and women? It is not the ruthless, the unbridled will; it is not freedom to do as one likes. That is the

---

[6] M. F. McNamara, 2,000 Famous Legal Quotations, 158 (1967).

[7] L. Hand, The Spirit of Liberty, in HANDBOOK FOR JUDGES 280, (G. Williams and K. Sampson, ed. 1984).

13

> denial of liberty, and leads straight to its
> overthrow.   A society in which men recognize
> no check upon their freedom soon becomes a
> society where freedom is the possession of
> only a savage few; as we have learned to our
> sorrow.   .

Those who so zealously seek to defend civil liberties

should be reminded that the greatest threat to liberty is

unrestrained, undisciplined freedom.   Neither education nor

government can function in a camp runamuck environment.

Americans are and should be a compassionate people, but we are

paying dearly for the irresponsible behavior of those who freely

do as they, or their consenting associates, please.   It is

nonsense to believe that the exercise of whatever one thinks of

as his/her "right" hurts no one else.   Some things do.

So, how did we go from where we were to where we are?

How did we change from our beginning precepts to the four myths?

Much of it came from Europe in the form of the enlightenment or

humanistic philosophies and in America with the development of

pragmatism.

Pragmatism is the only original American philosophy.

It finds what is good through human experience.   It looks to what

works best or what one thinks will work best.   Among the

developers of this philosophy were Oliver Wendell Holmes and John

Dewey.   Holmes was an outstanding jurist and writer, and he is

well-known for his statement that, "The life of the law has not

been logic: it has been experience."   Common Law I (1881).

Quite frankly, my own philosophy of law has been strongly

influenced by pragmatism and Dewey's "scientific method."   It has

also been influenced by Dean Roscoe Pound's theories of

"Sociological Jurisprudence," which involves the balancing of

14

conflicting interests. Pragmatism and sociological jurisprudence have many practical uses and applications in law, especially in judging and legislating.

Dewey was a philosopher and educator, and is known as the father of progressive education. He was named honorary president of the National Education Association in 1932, and in 1933, he was a chief designer and one of the signers of the Humanist Manifesto. At this point, humanism became a religion. The preamble of the Manifesto concludes:

> While this age does owe a vast debt to traditional religions, it is nonetheless obvious that any religion that can hope to be a synthesizing and dynamic force for today must be shaped for the needs of this age. To establish such a religion is a major necessity of the present. It is a responsibility which rests upon this generation.

Some of the tenets of the Manifesto read as follows:

> First: Religious humanists regard the universe as self-existing and not created.

> Second: Humanism believes that man is a part of nature and that he has emerged as the result of a continuous process.

>   . . .

> Fifth: Humanism asserts that the nature of the universe depicted by modern science makes unacceptable any supernatural or cosmic guarantees of human values.

There can be no doubt that humanism is a religion, it is based on evolution, and it rejects any supernatural God, the Bible, and Biblical morality. In other tenets, the Manifesto makes an open attack on the Church and Christians, it opposes the free enterprize system, and it advocates socialism. The Humanist Manifesto was originally published in the May/June 1933 issue of

15

APPENDIX B

<u>The New Humanist</u>. <u>See also</u>, <u>Humanist Manifestos I and II</u>, edited
by Paul Kurtz, Prometheus Books, Buffalo, NY.

These precepts began working their way into our public
schools--persistently and methodically--until finally the
education hierarchy, textbook writers and buyers, are
substantially indoctrinated. American History, civics, values,
and such subjects are being deconstructed and rewritten. Our
religious heritage is being systematically censored out of
existence in modern school texts.

Charles Francis Potter, another signer of the
Manifesto, and another honorary president of the N. E. A., wrote:

> Education is thus a most powerful ally
> of Humanism, and every American public school
> is a school of humanism. What can the
> theistic Sunday schools, meeting for an hour
> once a week, and teaching only a fraction of
> the children, do to stem the tide of a five-
> day program of humanistic teaching?[8]

The idea that public schools may not promote a religion is yet
another myth. "Secular humanism," atheism, and now to some
extent "new age," are the religions in American public schools.
Secular humanism is a recognized religion, and the same First
Amendment rights and limitations should be equally applicable to
it as to all religions. <u>Torcaso v. Watkins</u>, 367 U.S. 488 (1961).

A second Humanist Manifesto was published in the
September/October 1973 issue of <u>The Humanist</u>. Its preface reads
in part, "As in 1933, humanists still believe that traditional
theism, . . . is an unproved and outmoded faith." The new
Manifesto was divided into the subjects of Religion, Ethics, The
Individual, Democratic Society, World Community, and Humanity as

---

[8]   C. Potter, <u>Humanism: A New Religion</u>, 128 (1930).

16

a Whole. As to religion, nothing much was changed in attitude.
As to the subject of ethics, they wrote, "<u>Third</u>: We affirm that
moral values derive their source from human experience. Ethics
is <u>autonomous</u> and <u>situational</u>, needing no theological or
ideological sanction." Situation ethics is now certainly the
basis for the value system taught in public schools.

In the category of Democratic Society, they added a new
item which reads in part, "<u>Seventh</u>: . . . It also includes a
recognition of an individual's right to die with dignity,
euthanasia, and the right to suicide." The Manifesto also added
the following tenet, "<u>Ninth</u>: The separation of church and state
and the separation of ideology and state are imperatives."

I find this latter tenet to be somewhat puzzling.
Although the words "separation, church, and state" are not to be
found in the First Amendment, we know that Thomas Jefferson used
those words to assure the Danbury Baptists that the state would
not establish a religion. In this sense, he announced that there
was a "wall of separation." It is quite clear, however, that
that wall was one-way. There was never any intention to say that
morality should not be a part of government or of those who
govern. How one can separate ideology from the state is beyond
me, and that idea presents yet another myth. Every law
legislates someone's morality. Whenever a law is passed, one set
of beliefs is preferred over another, although not all laws
involve moral judgments. The idea that in a "pluralistic"
society all points of view are treated equally is unrealistic and
unworkable. A "pluralistic" society is simply one which is

17

APPENDIX B

making a transition from one controlling set of beliefs to
another controlling set.

I have no idea how much credence to put in one article
by one writer, but I found a shocker in an article published in
the January/February 1983 issue of <u>The Humanist</u>. Unfortunately,
it may reflect the true goals of humanist leaders. The title is
"A Religion for a New Age," and at page 26, John J. Dunphy
writes:

> I am convinced that the battle for
> humankind's future must be waged and won in
> the public school classroom by teachers who
> correctly perceive their role as the
> proselytizers of a new faith: a religion of
> humanity that recognizes and respects the
> spark of what theologians call divinity in
> every human being. These teachers must
> embody the same selfless dedication as the
> most rabid fundamentalist preachers, for they
> will be ministers of another sort, utilizing
> a classroom instead of a pulpit to convey
> humanist values in whatever subject they
> teach, regardless of the educational level--
> preschool day care or large state university.
> The classroom must and will become an arena
> of conflict between the old and the new--the
> rotting corpse of Christianity, together with
> all its adjacent evils and misery, and the
> new faith of humanism, resplendent in its
> promise of a world in which the never-
> realized Christian ideal of "love thy
> neighbor" will finally be achieved.

Hopefully, no Kentucky educator is promoting such.

It is difficult to find a daily newspaper or news
broadcast which does not contain some horror story about our
society or about the many problems in and with schools. In
schools, we have gone, in a short time, from problems with
talking and chewing gum to vandalism and shootings. We have gone
from a daily Bible reading, pledge to the flag, and prayer to the

18

189

distribution of condoms and you name it. People like the
Millers, the Martins, and the Thompsons (the appellants) want
something better for their children's education. But, unlike
some of our leaders, they do not have the means to provide it.
Government takes their taxes to support the public system, and
they are without the means to pay for an alternative.

Where can we go from here? Maybe it is time for some
good old "pragmatism." It is time to admit that the myths simply
do not work. Our "experience" with them has been bad, so a
change is needed.

A pragmatic decision which struck down segregated
schools served us well. Brown v. Bd. of Educ. of Topeka, 347
U.S. 483 (1954). Engle v. Vitale, 370 U.S. 421 (1962), which
struck down a state-sponsored prayer in public schools, cited no
precedent but relied on the fact that exposure to other children
reciting a prayer could psychologically damage an atheist. This,
too, was rather pragmatic.

Another recent application of some degree of pragmatism
came in the case of Barnes v. Glen Theater, Inc., 501 U.S. ___,
115 L.Ed.2d 504, 111 S.Ct. 2456 (1991). The case involved
Indiana's public indecency law which prohibited nude dancing as
entertainment. The Court had divided four-four on the question
of whether the statute violated the free expression clause of the
First Amendment. Although Justice Scalia determined, as one of
the plurality, that the statute was not even subject to First
Amendment scrutiny for various reasons, it was Justice Souter who
broke the tie. He held that although nude dancing was entitled
to some First Amendment protection, the state's reasons were not

19

190

merely moral grounds, but were to combat the secondary effects of prostitution and other criminal activity. As nude dancing would promote other prohibited conduct around the premises, the state had a right to prohibit it.

Although our case law and constitution prohibit any governmental activity which sponsors or promotes a particular religion--Christianity, Judaism, humanism, atheism, and new ageism included--there is no basis in law for government to be hostile to religion. As Justice Douglas wrote in <u>Zorach v. Clauson</u>, 343 U.S. 306, 313 (1952), "We are a religious people whose institutions presuppose a Supreme Being." Also, Justice Douglas wrote, "We find no constitutional requirement which makes it necessary for government to be hostile to religion and to throw its weight against efforts to widen the effective scope of religious influence." <u>Id.</u> at 314. Justice Black wrote, in <u>Everson v. Bd. of Educ. of Ewing Tp.</u>, 330 U.S. 1 (1947), the case which first applied the "wall of separation" to schools, "That Amendment [First] requires the state to be a neutral in its relations with groups of religious believers and non-believers; it does not require the state to be their adversary. State power is no more to be used so as to handicap religions, than it is to favor them." <u>Id.</u> at 18.

An air of neutrality is becoming more detectible. Three cases decided in 1993 reveal this. In <u>Zobrest v. Catalina Foothills School Dist.</u>, ___ U.S. ___, 113 S.Ct. 2462, 125 L.Ed.2d 1 (1993), the Court approved five-four the use of public funds to pay a sign language interpreter to aid a deaf student in a

20

Catholic high school. In <u>Lamb's Chapel v. Center Moriches Union Free School Dist.</u>, ___ U.S. ___, 113 S.Ct. 2141, 124 L.Ed.2d 352 (1993), the Court unanimously allowed the after-hours use of a public school by a church to show a film on raising a Christian family. The school was open for use by other groups. Finally, on November 9, 1993, the Court decided <u>Florence Co. School Dist. Four v. Carter</u>, ___ U.S. ___, 114 S.Ct. 361 (1993). The Court held that parents of a disabled child were entitled to state reimbursement when they withdrew their child from a public school which was not providing an "appropriate public education." The decision was based on the enabling legislation of 20 U.S.C. 1401(a)(18) and the Individuals with Disabilities Education Act.

The problems raised in this case are not merely moral or religious issues. They are economic issues. We must at least allow our young people and educators the academic freedom to consider "old fashioned" values. It is not necessary to erase from the teachings in public schools every Judeo-Christian principle on which this country was founded. There can and should at least be some balance of ideas and a fair and more level playing field. Even if one uses dialectics, with a thesis and an antithesis which then results in some synthesis; and if the current thesis is humanism, atheism, and new ageism; then, at least allow the antithesis of Biblical principles to come into the equation.

America has been thrust into world leadership, and our ability to fill that role will depend upon the education of our leaders. If our society is confused and out of control, and if

21

we do not understand what we are or what we should be, how can we possibly project a desirable image to the rest of the world? How can we project or defend our traditions and the beliefs which made us great, if we now abandon them and fail to educate our children regarding the foundations of our traditions? We are losing our source of strength. As Colson said, "We are separating the wheat from the chaff and keeping the chaff."

Our children must have a better opportunity for an education which will require the reestablishment of a learning environment with solid values. Better educated people work and produce better, and employers demand better educated employees; and not only that, employers must have employees with discipline and good character traits. We also need better education and a solid value system in order to combat crime and to cut our social costs due to immorality. Parents must again accept their responsibilities, and educators need to be given more latitude in controlling and disciplining the young people they must have in their school systems. It may well be that some revisions in the Juvenile Code will be required to accomplish any of this.

Although the appellants have lost this case, it may be that all is not yet lost. However, this Court is not in a position to order that any particular legislation be enacted or that any particular money be spent for the appellants' purposes. Nevertheless, some improvement in public education can be accomplished by the concerted efforts of parents, educators, legislators, executives, and lay leadership. Perhaps the greatest cause of concern for so many parents is that school

22

teaching often contradicts by indoctrination what parents wish to teach their children. Some serious examination must occur in text material, value lessons, teacher education, desired outcome-based objectives, methods of discipline, incentives for learning, and teaching students to think with less indoctrination, to mention a few. Hopefully, public education will become desirable.

In closing, it must be emphasized that time is of the essence. I am reminded of the story of the man who wanted to plant a type of tree he liked. When his gardner told him it would take over 100 years to mature, the owner replied, "Then plant it today. We've no time to waste."

23

†

ABOUT THE AUTHOR

J. William Howerton is a native and resident of Paducah, Kentucky, and was born in October 1931. He is a retired judge of the Kentucky Court of Appeals and served as chief judge from 1986 through 1990. He is a Korean veteran and a retired lieutenant colonel from the USAF Reserve. He graduated from the University of Kentucky with a BS in commerce and a Juris Doctor degree. He is presently chairman of a charitable foundation.

www.ingramcontent.com/pod-product-compliance
Lightning Source LLC
Chambersburg PA
CBHW020451130626
46549CB00001B/375